Praise for Dan Sherman's LinkedIn Training

"For over twenty years I've been guiding Fortune 500 companies with their marketing, and in that time I've never seen a more powerful tool for generating business and worldwide visibility than LinkedIn. My good friend Dan Sherman has now created what I consider to be an indispensible guide to using this powerful social media site to achieve all your professional goals. Read *Maximum Success with LinkedIn* today, and you will discover how to use the site to build any type of career or business that you want."
—**Charlie Cook, Marketing Coach, Author, and CEO of MarketingforSuccess.com.**

"It's a shame that so many people ignore LinkedIn as a viable career growth and business-building tool. Dan Sherman's *Maximum Success with LinkedIn* unlocks the secrets of how to use LinkedIn so that you can use it for your great benefit. A worthwhile guidebook for your success."
—**Jim F. Kukral, Author,** *Business Around a Lifestyle*

"Dan's book is an intelligent, easy-to-follow guide for anyone interested in benefiting from social media. I couldn't wait to log on to my LinkedIn account to implement a number of Dan's creative suggestions."
—**Ed Brodow, Author,** *Negotiation Boot Camp*

"It is no accident that Dan Sherman is one of the world's foremost authorities on LinkedIn. He studies, innovates, and educates around LinkedIn far beyond pretty much anyone on the planet. And in his phenomenally practical and readable book, *Maximum Success with LinkedIn*, Dan makes that passion and skill available to us mere mortals. If you're looking to develop You, Inc., this book should be your business bible. As Dan brilliantly puts it, "If you're not on LinkedIn, you're not in business!""
—**Rob Brown, Bestselling Author,** *How to Build Your Reputation*, **and Founder, Global Networking Council**

"I'm all about results, and Dan Sherman delivers in his book, which offers doable advice that is easy to understand and put into practice. If you are someone who needs to know how to use LinkedIn more powerfully for the professional side of your life, his book is a must read! I highly recommend it to my clients."
—**Sheryl Nicholson, CSP, International Speaker, Author, Coach**

"Dan Sherman has taken everything he has learned about how to use LinkedIn to build a worldwide brand and create the career of your dreams, and he's put it all in an easy step-by-step formula for you to use in your job search. Dan shows you how to rise to the top of recruiters' searches and showcase your skills and talents and how to get the recruiters to contact you to discuss their openings. I have bought numerous books on how to best use LinkedIn for finding a new job, but I now recommend Dan Sherman's *Maximum Success with LinkedIn* only because it takes you from beginner to expert in no time at all. Buy it, use it, and I guarantee it will open up so many new job search options it will leave you excited about working on your job search each day until you close on that new job."

—Frank Welzig, Executive Career Coach, and President, www.NewJobCoach.com

"This is one book you cannot afford to overlook! From beginning to end, *Maximum Success with LinkedIn* is a MUST READ. It outlines everything you need to know in order to propel your business miles ahead of your competitors and stay there."

—Terri Bork, Author, *The Google Places Bible*

"Dan Sherman is an expert on how to leverage LinkedIn to build your business connections beyond what you may have considered possible. In his book, *Maximum Success with LinkedIn*, he generously shares tips and strategies for expanding your LinkedIn connections and turning them into bankable leads. I highly recommend hiring Dan to educate and enlighten you or your employees on the true power of LinkedIn."

—Mandy Wildman, Money Momentum Coach, Monetize Your Vision Coaching

"I followed just a few of Dan's tips and took my LinkedIn connections from 400 to 1,400 from Friday to Monday with very little effort. I was actually out of town at a mastermind, so not spending much time at all online, but I still had a huge increase. I can't wait to see what happens when I really work at it! Thanks again for the training and the information you shared."

—Joanne Eckton, Management Consultant and Professional Coach

"Although my LinkedIn Profile was at 100% complete, I knew I was not utilizing the power of LinkedIn like I should be. I hired Dan for a one-on-one session to teach me how to optimize my profile, add applications, and learn the value of the paid version. Dan was excellent at staying on task and teaching me in 90 minutes what would have taken me 20 hours to figure out on my own. I'll use Dan's expertise for my clients in the near future. Thanks, Dan!"

—Clint Babcock, Vice President, Sandler Sales Training

"I went to one of Dan's presentations on the power of LinkedIn and employed some of the tactics he taught about beefing up your profile. I own a fishing charter website, and now if you type "fishing" or "fishing charters" in the People Search, I am number one! Dan's tactics and methods for business growth generate immediate results."

—Chad Nikolic CEO, FishNCheap.com

"Dan knows his stuff. I went to a recent class where Dan took people from 0 to 60 regarding how to leverage LinkedIn for their business. They may have come in knowing nothing, but after two hours they had everything they needed to know how to effectively market themselves and to generate leads using LinkedIn."

—Mark Guthrie, Chief E-architect and Owner, biz360.biz

"My company just went through a rebranding, and so I came to Dan to learn how to post videos on my LinkedIn profile. He showed me how, and also taught me how to join groups and which ones to join, which I had no clue about. His training will help my business tremendously."

—Jan Tinder, Group Vice President, The Advantage Group

"I knew nothing about LinkedIn before I came to Dan's training, and I was very skeptical about how I would use it to benefit my business. Dan knows LinkedIn inside and out, and now I'm totally confident that I'm going to get a lot of leads from the site in terms of people finding me, and because of my ability to find other people. I'm going to really start to connect with others and grow my business. If you want to learn LinkedIn, get in touch with Dan."

—Robert Case, Commercial Lender, Signature Capital Lending

"If you've not had the opportunity to hear and learn from Dan about LinkedIn, you're missing out on great information that can significantly boost your B2B and B2C business. Dan is an absolute expert when it comes to maximizing your presence on LinkedIn. I highly recommend Dan as a speaker, seminar leader, and consultant."

—Andre Kasberger, Online Marketing Strategist

"Dan convinced me and showed me how to use LinkedIn effectively. On previous occasions I found LinkedIn difficult to use and purposeless, so I canceled my account. Dan changed my mind, and within a half an hour I had all the basic tools to effectively set up a profile and start collecting contacts again that were relevant to my business. Dan is fantastic! In fact, I happened to run into two of my contacts today, and we opened a productive dialogue. Without LinkedIn, those conversations would have never taken place. The net result is I will be doing business with these people in the next couple of days."

—Philip Frommholz, Owner, Phil the Mover

"Dan's presentation on LinkedIn was filled with the nuts-and-bolts information I needed to start improving my LinkedIn profile, which I expect will lead to many opportunities to connect with other professionals. I recommend his workshop to anyone, whether you are a beginner or a more advanced LinkedIn user."

—Joe "The Blog Guy" Jacobson, Owner, Step By Step Blog Building

"I attended Dan's LinkedIn class, and it was really helpful. I already had a LinkedIn account, but didn't really "get it" and in fact was a little put off by the whole thing.

But Dan took us through using LinkedIn step by step, showing how to optimize our profiles, the importance of groups and discussions, etc. Now when I do a search on my specialty keywords, I'm on the first page. Great course, great value."

—Mark Liquorman, Microsoft Access Expert

"I signed up for Dan's LinkedIn class because he is a LinkedIn expert! Dan has taken the time to … master LinkedIn, [and] he is a patient teacher and has obviously provided training to attendees of all skills and experience levels. Dan Sherman is a great LinkedIn trainer, I can definitely recommend his classes to anyone looking to learn how to begin using LinkedIn or to optimize their profile and leverage this incredibly valuable business building tool."

—Amy Campbell, Marketing Consultant

"Though I have been an active member of the LinkedIn community for some time, I found Dan's training to be highly informative and valuable. Dan presents his subject matter in an engaging and easy-to-understand manner. If you are looking for ways to leverage LinkedIn to grow your business, you must contact Dan Sherman."

—Lee Silverstein, Executive Career Coach, TampaBayJobCoach.com

"Dan provides an outstanding, detailed synopsis of not only the many facets of LinkedIn, but also how to get found, how to find others and broaden your net of exposure. Dan's training really opened my eyes to a lot of areas of LinkedIn to help expose my business, create partnerships, and find clients. Highly recommended."

—Jay Adams, President, Alpha Omega Telecom, Inc.

"Just finished Dan's LinkedIn training, and I definitely feel that I'm walking away with a lot of information that will help me. I wasted a lot of time in the past on the site, and now I feel like my time will be spent more fruitfully. I'm excited to get on LinkedIn, try some things, and practice."

—Victor Amuso, Software Developer, ParableSoft

"I attended Dan Sherman's LinkedIn training, and I learned exactly what I needed to use LinkedIn to take my business to the next level. Dan is really a LinkedIn expert. Not only is he very involved on LinkedIn, but he is also a very great teacher. He really helps you no matter what your level of LinkedIn expertise. I strongly recommend Dan if you need a LinkedIn expert to help your company."

—Paul Belshaw, Owner, Belshaw Accounting and Tax Services

"I wanted to learn to use LinkedIn to grow my business. That's when I discovered Dan Sherman, and my search was basically over. I've learned more—and learned more quickly—from Dan's courses than from anyone else. With many years of marketing experience under his belt, Dan is a true pro. He not only knows how to apply tried-and-true marketing principles to the new world of Internet marketing, he has immersed himself in the details of LinkedIn. And, unlike so many other 'experts' in these areas, Dan really knows how to teach important principles and techniques to newbies and veterans alike."

—Luke Melton, Graphic Designer, Latitude 28 Design and Marketing

"Until I took Dan's LinkedIn course, I had no idea what it could do for my business. His class was informative, thorough, and easy to understand. Dan provides hands-on instruction that works for both the novice and seasoned user. He has an incredible, in-depth knowledge of LinkedIn as well as other marketing strategies. I highly recommend his book and classes with complete confidence."

—Terie Hynish, Unit Leader, PartyLite

"I have personally worked with Dan and attended his excellent LinkedIn seminars. Dan excels at staying on top of new technologies and is a great teacher and coach in several areas, including social media marketing and especially LinkedIn. I highly recommend Dan."

—Tony Rockliff, Chief Executive Officer, BestInternetMarketingSecrets.org

"I am so glad that I attended Dan Sherman's LinkedIn seminar and can't wait to put into practice all that I learned from him. He is extremely knowledgeable and proficient in the world of social media—so much so that I only wish we had more time together. I will definitely be attending future LinkedIn courses of Dan's and would highly recommend others do the same."

—Lisa Keeling, Business Consultant, XL411.com

"I attended a LinkedIn class with Dan Sherman and found the information very compelling; so much so that I'm going to go home right now and start updating my connections and my profile all in an effort to increase my business, my sales, and my bottom line. I recommend you learn from Dan."

—Don Fisher, Multimedia Business Consultant

"I thought that LinkedIn was just about jobs and my résumé, and that's all I had on there. Before I took Dan's training, I never had any idea what it could do for my business, not only for marketing to other online marketers, but also to my community of wholesale clothing stores, manufacturers, and Zumba enthusiasts. I found lots of ways to find groups and companies, and how to market my business. I learned a lot from Dan."

—Vijay Harkishnani, Entrepreneur and Zumba Instructor

"Dan Sherman is truly a wealth of information on LinkedIn. He is a dynamic public speaker who can take any business owner from a place of very little social media marketing knowledge to a point where they are ready to begin the very next day, promoting their personal and business brands throughout the social media world. He has extensive knowledge of all phases of LinkedIn and social media marketing. Dan can teach you step by step so you are not overwhelmed with the idea of using technology to market your business, and that is so important for business owners as well as entrepreneurs today. I highly recommend Dan Sherman."

—Dr. Kytka Hilmar-Jezek, Bestselling Author

"Dan's knowledge and skill in the area of LinkedIn and social media is exceptional. I found that he gets results swiftly and conveys his know-how with simplicity, which is a rare huge plus. I highly recommend Dan to any company owner or entrepreneur needing and expecting to work with a pro to help them acquire a continued high volume of Internet traffic."

—Joe Yazbeck, President, Prestige Leader Development

"I recently attended one of Dan's LinkedIn seminars and was blown away with the insightful information he was able to share. I realized I had not been using LinkedIn to its full potential for maximum exposure, not only on the LinkedIn site, but SEO benefits as well. I've immediately implemented the changes on my profile and would recommend that everyone do the same. If you are in the business of building connections and being found, you won't realize the full potential until you take one of Dan's classes. Thanks again, Dan!"

—Rae Catanese, Blogger and Realtor

"My husband and I had the pleasure of attending Dan's LinkedIn seminar at Barcamp in Sarasota this past weekend. Dan really impressed upon us the value of LinkedIn and showed us how to maximize our LinkedIn accounts to generate business and potential clients. Dan is truly the LinkedIn expert and knows LinkedIn like no other. I highly recommend any businessperson to take Dan's class and learn about LinkedIn. I would even go as far as to say, it could make the difference between whether or not your business can survive and thrive! Thank you, Dan!"

—Julie Larson, Web Designer and Internet Marketer

"I have heard Dan speak several times on LinkedIn and was really impressed with his knowledge and his ability to share this knowledge with beginners like me. I was blown away with his knowledge base. Dan is an asset to any business, big or small, who wishes to make a presence in the social marketing arena. I would say hire him today."

—Jan Stammer, Owner, Circle of Independence

"Dan is truly the LinkedIn expert. Dan explained the process and organization for this site clearly and concisely. I am very excited to be participating on LinkedIn now. Get your business moving more effectively with good connections. Hire Dan, the LinkedIn expert so you can get more business. Thank you, Dan!"

—Susan Higley, RDH, LMT

"I just finished Dan Sherman's training on LinkedIn. I learned how to save thousands of dollars in consulting every year, and that's just one of the benefits I got out of it. I highly recommend his training."

—Jim Thornton, Founder, Leadership for Continuous Improvement

"I had the pleasure to meet Dan through one of his many great webinars about efficient use of LinkedIn for professional branding. Dan's online training was of great value and filled with new learning, suggestions, and techniques even for advanced LinkedIn users. I will personally be looking forward to other webinars from Dan and strongly recommend attending."

—A. Albeshelani, Manager, Production Management at Nuance Communications

"Thanks, Dan—excellent online training and a very good use of my time. Your well-organized LinkedIn training was informative, interactive, and even better made me aware of several 'hidden' aspects of LinkedIn functionality. I highly recommend anyone using LinkedIn to listen to this session. What a wonderful resource LinkedIn offers once you get to know its hidden features."

—Ken James, Television Technologist

"I enjoyed listening to Dan's BRILLIANT online training on LinkedIn. I use LinkedIn every single day and thought I knew all there was to know about LinkedIn. Sequentially and strategically, Dan swiftly cuts through the nonsense and gets to the point, giving you the ammunition needed to fire up your profiles."

—Kamlesh Darji, Life Optimization Coach

"When we needed a LinkedIn expert to contribute to our internationally read marketing blog, we reached out to one of the best in the business, Dan Sherman. He's now our go-to expert on all subjects related to LinkedIn, including how to use the site to build your business and create a worldwide brand. The response to Dan's posts has been great, as our readers really appreciate his practical and easy-to-implement advice. Thanks, Dan, for helping our clients become LinkedIn Superstars!"

—Lauren Johnson, Marketing and Affiliate Manager

"I was fortunate enough to book Dan to speak at the organization I run called Tampa Bay Computer Society on using LinkedIn to grow your business, and he was sensational. The strategies he taught our members will help them gain more customers and more sales in a short amount of time. Dan is a LinkedIn expert, and his ability to explain LinkedIn in a way that everyone benefits is fantastic; both veteran Internet marketers and newbies alike were really impressed and grateful. I strongly endorse Dan as a LinkedIn trainer to any company or organization looking to create rapid success using LinkedIn."

—Dave Dockery, Founder, Tampa Bay Computer Society

"I've attended two of Dan Sherman's LinkedIn Trainings and look forward to more. Dan has taught me a great deal about how to achieve my goals using LinkedIn. Dan is a LinkedIn expert who knows how to explain the site in clear details, so that anyone can immediately put to use his advice and expand their presence."

—David Mitchell Blood, Green Entrepreneur

"Dan is not only a LinkedIn expert but also an extremely engaging trainer. I've viewed his online training (10 Ways to Find Your Perfect Job on LinkedIn) several times and plan to play it again. Yes, it's that good. Thanks for the work you do, Dan. It helps me do my work better."

—Christine Osborne, Encore Navigator

"I had the pleasure recently to work with Dan to moderate his online training: 10 Ways to Find Your Perfect Job on LinkedIn. I agree that Dan Sherman is truly a LinkedIn expert, and the LinkedIn Training he provided was very well received. Dan's approach to LinkedIn Training is clear, concise, and he is very genuine and sincere about helping each individual maximize the power of LinkedIn. His Linked-In Training warrants reviewing and watching it again, as he has proven himself to be the LinkedIn expert that I was looking for. He was able to help so many, and I highly recommend taking advantage of his special offers."

—Mark Lynch, Senior Director of Business Development, ILostMyJob.com.

"Dan Sherman is a great teacher on how to use LinkedIn. I am very excited with what we have accomplished on my profile. Dan taught me how my profile should look: add recommendation letters that were hard copy only and, most important, how to connect with people. It's only been two weeks since our first session, and I have two interviews. This is what I call success, and it's all due to Dan's teaching ability and my follow thru. Thanks again, Dan."

—Theresa Kuhn, Executive Assistant

"Dan is the true definition of LinkedIn expert. He was able to answer all the questions that I had. He is patient and insightful to what my needs were. I enjoyed working with Dan and would be happy to recommend him to whoever is seeking help with their career."

—John Micchelli, Sales Professional

"I had the benefit of attending a LinkedIn webinar offered by Dan. His insights led me to update my own LinkedIn profile, and I seem to get more response now. Dan's webinar also led me to modify a LinkedIn skills-building session I facilitated at one of my networking groups the next day. Looks like I turned to Dan and his expertise just in time!"

—Wolfgang Koch, Career Services Specialist

MAXIMUM
SUCCESS

—— WITH ——

Linkedin

MAXIMUM SUCCESS

SUCCESS

WITH

Linkedin

Dominate Your Market, Build
a Global Brand, and Create
the Career of Your Dreams

DAN SHERMAN

New York   Chicago   San Francisco   Lisbon   London
Madrid   Mexico City   New Delhi   San Juan
Seoul   Singapore   Sydney   Toronto

3 4 5 6 7 8 9 10   QFR/QFR   1 8 7 6 5 4 3

ISBN   978-0-07-181233-7
MHID   0-07-181233-4

e-ISBN   978-0-07-181234-4
e-MHID   0-07-181234-2

Library of Congress Cataloging-in-Publication Data

Sherman, Dan, 1956-
    Maximum success with LinkedIn / by Dan Sherman.
      p. cm.
    Includes index.
    ISBN 978-0-07-181234-4 (alk. paper)—ISBN 0-07-181234-2 (alk. paper)   1. LinkedIn (Electronic resource)   2. Business networks—Computer network resources.   3. Internet marketing.   4. Online social networks.   I. Title.
    HD69.S8S535 2013
    658.8'72—dc23   2012036263

McGraw-Hill books are available at special quantity discounts to use as premiums and sales promotions or for use in corporate training programs. To contact a representative, please e-mail us at bulksales@mcgraw-hill.com.

This book is printed on acid-free paper.

Contents

Author's Note   **xi**

Preface   **xiii**

Introduction: Love at First Click   **xv**
Internet Databases Are in My Blood   xvi
How to Create a Yacht   xvii

Chapter 1: Social Media Is Not Your Father's Marketing   **1**
Honesty Is King   2
LinkedIn: Your Personal Worldwide Database   3
Who's Having Success with LinkedIn?   4
Understanding the LinkedIn Levels   5

Chapter 2: The LinkedIn Profile: Your Miniwebsite   **7**
Creating a Powerful Profile   7
How to Make Your Profile Rock!   8
Designing the Perfect Information Box   9
Creating the Ad for You, Inc.   15
Adding Sections That Make Your Profile Shine   25

Chapter 3: What Goes Around:
Giving and Getting Recommendations   **29**
Social Proof Is the Key to Success   30
Getting Recommendations from First-Level Connections   31
Want More Recommendations? Write Some!   34
Know Who You Are Recommending   36
Manage Your Recommendations   37
Get the Social Proof You Need   38

Chapter 4: It's Showtime! Adding Applications for a Multimedia Profile — 41

Blogs — 42
SlideShare — 43
Box.net — 44
Reading List by Amazon — 46
Events — 47
Polls — 47
Jazz Up Your Profile with Cool Applications — 48

Chapter 5: The Finishing Touches: Creating a Rocking Profile — 51

Skills & Expertise — 51
Languages — 53
Education — 54
Contact — 55
Personal Information — 57

Chapter 6: All About Keywords: Optimizing Your Profile to Be Found — 59

Four Required Places for Your Keywords — 60
Research Your Competitors — 62
Advanced Optimization Strategies — 62
Where *Not* to Optimize Your Profile — 64
Moving Sections in Your Profile — 65

Chapter 7: Your Virtual Rolodex: Grow Your Network by Adding Contacts — 67

500 Is the Magic Number — 68
To Connect or Not to Connect — 69
How to Get More Connections — 69
Avoid the Dreaded *Report Spam* — 70
How to Start Inviting Contacts — 71
Creative Ways to Get More Connections — 73
Open Networkers: The Key to Hypergrowth — 76
Getting a Paid Open Networking Account — 77

Chapter 8: Your Social Influence Circle: Searching For and Contacting People   **81**

Using Advanced People Search   82
Save Your Search   85
Making a Personal Connection   86
Contacting Non-First-Level Connections   88
Reaching a Second-Level Connection   89
Reaching a Third-Level Connection   91
Contacting Groups of People   92
Tag, You're It—Grouping Contacts   94
Messaging More than 50 People   95
Finding a Mentor on LinkedIn   96

Chapter 9: Power in Tribes: Joining and Creating Groups   **103**

Joining Groups   104
Diversify Your Groups   105
Navigating Your Groups   107
Messaging Group Members   109
Leaving a Group   110
Creating a Group   110
Promoting Your Group   113
Creating Subgroups for More Influence   114
Building Your Business with a Group   114
Getting Group Members Engaged   120
Building Website Traffic with Groups   120

Chapter 10: Give to Get: Answering and Asking Questions   **123**

How to Answer Questions   123
Asking Questions   126
How to Ask Questions   127
Brand Yourself with Questions   129
Your Answer Command Center   130
Extending Your Question Longer   131
Sharing Your Questions   131

Contents

**Chapter 11: Promoting Yourself and Your Company
with Events**   **133**
Creating an Event   133
Publicizing Your Event   135
Advanced Strategies for Events   136

**Chapter 12: Good Company:
Adding Your Company and Following Others**   **139**
Listing Your Company   139
Adding Details About Your Company   141
Creating a Company Status Update   144
Make Your Company Page Exciting   145
Prospecting for Business Using Companies   146
Contacting People at Your Target Company   147
Using Introductions for Prospecting   148
Leveraging Company Information   149
Follow That Company   150
Use Company Pages to Create Opportunities   151

**Chapter 13: Off to Work We Go:
Finding Your Perfect Job**   **155**
Why LinkedIn Crushes Job Boards   156
Get the Low-Hanging Fruit First   159
Searching Paid Job Listings   160
Searching for Jobs in the Companies Section   162
Looking for Jobs in Groups   163
Turn Your Profile into a Job-Hunting Machine   164
Advanced Profile Tips for Job Hunters   165
Leverage Your Alma Mater   169
Find a Job Fair   170
Participate in Groups   170
Answer Questions to Establish Your Brand   171
Search on Your Specialty   172
Upgrade to a Job Seeker Premium Account   172
Do Research for Your Interview   173
Social Media Job-Hunting Advice from a Career Coach   173

Chapter 14: Laser Focus Your Searches
Using LinkedIn Signal   **179**
    Find a Job with Signal   179
    Build Your Business with Signal   181

Chapter 15: Going Mobile: The Power of LinkedIn
on the Go   **183**
    You *Can* Take It with You   183
    LinkedIn Is for Tablets Too   185

Chapter 16: The Daily Approach to Success on
LinkedIn   **187**
    Making the Most of Status Updates   187
    LinkedIn Etiquette Regarding Updates   189
    Clever Ways to Show Up in Network Updates   189
    Create a LinkedIn Goal Statement   190
    Powerful Daily Success Activities   191
    Turbocharged LinkedIn Success Activities   194

Conclusion: Opportunity Is Knocking
at Your Door   **197**
    People Buy People   200
    Measure Your Success   201

Appendix A: LinkedIn Success Blueprints   **203**

Appendix B: Successful Selling in the Age of
Social Media   **219**
    The New Five-Step Sales Process   220
    Put Your Clients' Needs First   221
    The Art of Giving   222

For More Information   **225**

Index   **227**

Author's Note

Anyone with at least a casual acquaintance with the Internet knows that it is a constantly evolving, rapidly innovating space to work and play. New developments in technology and changes to websites happen minute-by-minute. That's what makes the Internet so exciting. In this book, I've given you all the latest information on LinkedIn that was current at press time. As the inevitable changes take place on the site, I will be providing regular updates to the book through the following website:

www.mhprofessional.com/sherman

Preface

I'm excited about LinkedIn. I truly believe in its potential to uncover hidden opportunities for every working man and woman in the world. Anyone who takes the time to explore LinkedIn can find opportunities to grow their business, gain worldwide publicity, land the perfect career, develop a network of referral partners, meet mentors who will take their career to the next level, locate investors for their ideas, and much more.

I tell everyone I meet about LinkedIn, and often I'm greeted with phrases like, "Well, I have a profile, but I have not done much with it," or "I received some invitations but never joined ... couldn't figure out what it was about."

Why people have avoided using LinkedIn is understandable for three reasons. One, the constraints on our time limit how much we can take in, and unless people truly see the benefit, they are not going to get involved. Two, since LinkedIn is a "social network," businesspeople might dismiss it as a waste of time, just another place to play games and chitchat about the weather and TV shows. Three, LinkedIn is considered to be exclusively a site for posting your résumé and looking for a job

I wrote this book to convince you that while LinkedIn is a social network and it's great for finding a job, it really is an all-purpose, high-powered professional networking site where you can accomplish all of your business goals. I want all businesspeople to stop what they are doing, log on to LinkedIn, and start making the connections that will take their career—and their life—to the next level.

After reading this book, you will know everything you need to know to make the most of LinkedIn, and then it's up to you to put the largest professional networking site on the planet to work for you. I hope you find this book inspiring and educational, and that you put these techniques to work right away.

As with any Internet-based resource, LinkedIn constantly evolves. There will undoubtedly be changes to the site and I suspect even more great features added as time goes on. That's why I encourage you to visit my site, www.LinkedSuccess.com, where you will find information about updates to LinkedIn, online training courses, downloadable articles, and other resources to help you use the site to achieve all your goals.

Lastly, I would like to acknowledge Anton Graphics, Inc., for their help in creating the images for the interior of the book (www.anton-graphics.com).

To Your LinkedIn Success!
Dan Sherman

Introduction: Love at First Click

My involvement with LinkedIn began because of a habit. It's a habit that I freely admit to, I'm not ashamed of it, and I don't want to cure this habit. In fact, I like this habit: I'm a reader.

I love to read. Fiction, nonfiction, whatever I can get my hands on. To me, libraries are like temples full of the most amazing knowledge and entertainment right there for me to enjoy—and they're free! My library is one of my favorite places. You will find me most weekends trudging out of my local library with an armload of books.

I also loved to read as a teen, and when I went off to college I majored in English, which meant I got to indulge in my habit for four solid years, reading the best literature the world has produced. Reading and writing papers on what I read ... that was indeed the life. This could be why I graduated with honors, even though my minor was in backgammon and it seems I spent an inordinate amount of time participating in that addictive game.

Today I enjoy reading all kinds of books. I enjoy fiction—I'm a Clive Cussler and Michael Crichton junkie—but I tend to gravitate to business books. I've devoured everything Richard Branson, the daredevil CEO of Virgin (and one of my first-level LinkedIn connections), has put on paper. I have studied books about the creation of Starbucks, Apple, McDonald's, the Republic of Tea, and other corporate success stories. I've devoured motivational books by Tony Robbins, Brian Tracy, Jack Canfield, and Joe Vitale: anything that would inspire me and help me grow professionally has landed on my reading list.

My love of reading also extends to magazines, and for as long as I can remember I have subscribed to and read faithfully six magazines: *Forbes, Fortune, Inc., Fast Company, Entrepreneur*, and *Wired*. Every month I read them cover to cover, and I always find something of value to add to my business education. My files are bulging with torn-out articles from these magazines about new trends, products, websites, or companies I need to research.

And so it happened on that fateful day in 2007 when the latest copy of *Inc.* landed in my mailbox. I opened it breathlessly in anticipation of reading yet another fantastic tale of an entrepreneur shooting for the moon, living his or her dream, or starting the next Apple or Microsoft. I was not disappointed, for in that issue was a story about a four-year-old website that was taking the business world by storm, a site that was connecting the world's professionals into a massive online networking database.

The site was called LinkedIn. I read every word in that article and felt a strange tingling in my body ... no, it was not the onset of a cold. It was the realization that what I had waited my entire professional life for was here. I immediately jumped on my Dell laptop, opened an account, filled out a profile, and started inviting friends and creating groups. From day one I became a fanatic and never looked back.

Internet Databases Are in My Blood

I think the reason I had such a strong affinity to LinkedIn was that I was no stranger to Internet databases that help people create connections to propel their careers forward. In fact, I used to sell them.

During the boom years of the Internet bubble (the late 1990s and early 2000s), I was director of marketing at two Internet companies in Silicon Valley: Personic and BrassRing Systems. At both firms we sold applicant tracking software to human resources departments at large companies, in a category then called ASP, or Application Service Provider. We sold a hosted service, meaning the software sat on computers in our facilities while the end user—a human resources staffer—simply logged on and utilized the program to find the best candidates for open positions from the résumés he or she had collected. Today this kind of software is known by newer names, including SaaS (software as a service) and cloud computing.

Since I had been a firm believer in the idea and the primary cheerleader at two companies that sold hosted databases in the recruiting industry, the concept of LinkedIn was a no-brainer: you log on and there are all your contacts. No muss, no fuss, no software to install, debug, or maintain.

Fast-forward to today, and I have become a social media trainer who teaches business owners how to make the most of LinkedIn, a social media site praised by Nielsen Online as "the world's largest audience of affluent influential professionals." For me personally, LinkedIn has brought many rewards:

- I have a network of 23 million businesspeople I can ask questions of and get advice.
- I get consulting offers and media requests regularly because of my daily presence on the site.
- I have built a personal brand as an social media expert through my interactions on LinkedIn and with my groups.
- I get training requests from groups and companies that wish to learn how to learn to use LinkedIn.

In short, I use this amazing site to create the kind of life I always wanted. And now I want to show you how to use LinkedIn to get anything you want, for it truly is a remarkable "manifesting" device. Whatever you need, you can produce it on LinkedIn.

How to Create a Yacht

I love reading positive-thinking books, such as Rhonda Byrne's *The Secret*, Esther and Jerry Hicks's *The Law of Attraction*, and Joe Vitale's *The Attractor Factor*. I agree that you attract to you that which you think about. And to me, LinkedIn is a real-life wish-granting dream generator that will send to you whatever you hope to create.

Let me share with you one example. A good friend of mine lives in my hometown of Tampa, Florida, and she loves to go boating. Now, Tampa is a boat-crazy town; every weekend people take to their boats and set sail into the crystalline waters of the Gulf of Mexico, but my friend had no boat, nor did any of her friends.

But she had LinkedIn, she loved it, and she was good at using the site. She had started a LinkedIn group for power users in Tampa who also loved LinkedIn and were dedicated to building large personal networks on the site. One day she decided she wanted to throw a party for her group and the party should be on a yacht. Not a small yacht, either. Something grand.

So she logged onto LinkedIn and did an investigation in the Advanced People Search. She used the keyword *yacht*, typed in the Tampa zip code, and hit the *Submit* button. The results returned three yacht brokers in her network. She reached out to the brokers and told them about her group (of which I am a member), how they were influential decision makers, movers and shakers, and so on, and how the yacht brokers would benefit by aligning their business with her group of LinkedIn power users.

One yacht broker liked the idea, and so he and she met in person. That's how it came to be that the first party for her LinkedIn group was held on a 50-foot yacht on the gulf. The broker was the party's sponsor, and he got to display one of his yachts for sale while my friend reciprocated by getting the word out through LinkedIn and other social media sites about the broker's company and all the wonderful floating pleasure palaces he had for sale.

That's just one tale of many. There are so many people who are finding jobs, partners, investors, mentors, employees ... even yachts ... on LinkedIn. So let's get going, and I will show you how you too can find whatever you want and achieve all of your goals on LinkedIn.

Chapter 1: Social Media Is Not Your Father's Marketing

Before we jump right into LinkedIn, it's important to lay down a few ground rules about marketing yourself in social media. It will help you approach LinkedIn the right way and get the best results. I want to help you avoid being "that guy"...the person who is shunned by people at networking events because he shows up and immediately starts tossing out his business cards like he's dealing Texas Hold 'em in a Vegas card room. You need to approach marketing on social media with some finesse and restraint.

Let's start at the beginning: I've been in marketing well over 20 years, working in Silicon Valley, as I mentioned, and also for large corporations like Charles Schwab. I've been in the advertising game since I graduated from Tufts University in the Boston suburbs with a degree in English and got a job at an advertising agency as a copywriter.

The changes that social media has brought to the world of advertising and marketing have been nothing short of earth-shattering. No longer are marketers held hostage to TV, radio, and newspapers for presenting their wares to the world. With the push of a button and click of the mouse, anyone can send a marketing message via video, post, tweet, update, blog entry, and more around the world in an instant.

In short, marketing has been revolutionized. What does this have to do with you? Well, you are marketing a product called You, Inc.

You will notice on LinkedIn that the site revolves primarily around people, not companies (there is a section for building a company profile, which we'll examine later). As you market You, Inc. on social media sites like LinkedIn, you need to pay heed to the new rules, because marketing today is a brave new world.

We used to have traditional marketing, or interruption marketing, where marketers would break into your Steelers game or *American Idol* episode and bark at you with some ridiculous commercial. (This still happens, but technology has invented so many ways, like TiVo, to avoid it.) Now we have social media marketing, which is in essence a conversation. Specifically on LinkedIn, social media marketing is a dialogue you have with the people you want to influence to, among other things:

- Hire you
- Work for you
- Invest in your company
- Be your mentor
- Partner with you

So you need to think soft sell, not hard sell. You can equate marketing on social media sites like LinkedIn to a backyard barbecue. Now, you would never walk up to a stranger at a barbecue and say, "Hi, can I sell you some insurance?" You get the point. Social media is all about engaging people in conversations, getting them interested in you first, and then seeing if there is some common ground for doing business as a next step.

Honesty Is King

Essentially, visiting a social media portal is just like attending a party where you let people get to know you and then invite them to learn more about you by visiting your site or blog, where you provide more information on how you can help them. Marketing on social media sites like LinkedIn means being real, authentic, and honest. People buy from those they know, like, and trust, and in social media you have the opportunity to let people see how much you know and let them make up their own minds that you're someone they need to do business with.

The old saying (attributed to many people, including Zig Ziglar, the granddaddy of sales training) is "people don't care how much you know, until they know how much you care." With social media marketing, you show people that you care about them by being interested in them, asking questions, and offering help. Then you move on to creating a business relationship.

Fortunately, LinkedIn has extensive ways for you to create situations where people can get to know, like, and trust you. It's a great place to become a valuable resource to people by expressing your expertise through group discussions, through the Answers feature, and by presenting your knowledge in videos, blog posts, Power-Points, PDFs, presentations, and more that you add to your profile using LinkedIn's free applications.

Social media is a "pull" medium as opposed to a "push" one. You use LinkedIn's powerful features to show professionals from around the world your expertise and pull them into your sphere. It goes without saying that it's not the place for the spam or trickery that sometimes is associated with a certain rogue element found in the Internet marketing world (e.g., the folks who have you click on a link purporting to take you to a cool site that instead takes you to a male enhancement drug advertisement). LinkedIn is a place where you can build your brand as an expert and have people knocking on your door...and what's simply amazing is that it's free! Yes, there are premium accounts, which we'll cover, but I would say that 90 percent of the world can achieve its goals with the free basic account.

With that disclaimer about marketing on social media out of the way (be nice, play fair, don't be pushy—not too hard, right?), let's take a closer look at marketing You, Inc. on LinkedIn.

LinkedIn: Your Personal Worldwide Database

There are plenty of social media sites to join, but none will have the immediate impact that LinkedIn will on your professional career.

You can play Farmville and Mafia Wars on Facebook or watch Lady Gaga and silly cat videos on YouTube, but you can achieve tremendous success on LinkedIn, and that's why it's growing at an astounding rate. LinkedIn has 175 million members right now and is growing fast by adding two users per second.

The best thing about LinkedIn is that it has the most affluent, most well-connected users of any social media site. Executives from all Fortune 500 companies are registered on LinkedIn, and 66 percent of LinkedIn's members are decision makers or have influence in the purchase decisions for their companies. LinkedIn holds the record for the highest average household income over all other social networking sites at over $109,000 per member!

While you can plant imaginary crops or wink at potential mates on other sites, LinkedIn is all business. There are no distractions. On LinkedIn you will find professionals who are focused on one thing only: networking to create success for themselves and their businesses. LinkedIn is no longer a secret; with its IPO in 2011 valuing it at over $6 billion, everyone now knows about LinkedIn. In 2011, even America's president joined the LinkedIn phenomenon by holding an online town meeting to talk about his economic proposals.

Who's Having Success with LinkedIn?

LinkedIn helps professionals across the board. Although many people at first considered it to be a job-hunting site, it is so much more than that. The range of people that the site helps is quite extensive:

- Consultants who want to connect with prospective clients and build up their brand equity as experts
- Business-to-business marketers creating awareness of their new product launches or service offerings
- Sales professionals who do research on prospects before contacting them, finding out personal interests, school affiliations, and whom they might know in common in an effort to create better rapport

- Job hunters expanding their circles of business contacts to both create a better chance of finding that perfect job and keep themselves top of mind with potential employers
- Small businesses staying in front of customers and reaching out to prospects
- Entrepreneurs seeking funding who are getting the attention of investors in their ideas
- Recruiters looking to find staff for their companies and sorting through the world's largest pool of talent

Basically, anyone in business can get a boost from the global networking capabilities of LinkedIn. I tell my consulting clients flat out: if you are not on LinkedIn, you are not in business.

LinkedIn offers you the platform to achieve all your business goals, including:

- Driving more traffic to your sites
- Getting media attention
- Promoting your events
- Finding the perfect work
- Interacting with professionals from around the globe you would never have been able to contact before
- Obtaining free advice from top consultants on urgent business issues

Understanding the LinkedIn Levels

Any discussion on how to leverage LinkedIn should begin with its overall structure. Your connections on LinkedIn are made up of the people you invite to join your network and, by degrees, all the people in the networks of those directly linked to you. Say you invite Sally, who works with you, into your network. She becomes your first-degree connection. You and Sally might have other first-degree connections in common, since you may both have invited other colleagues into your networks.

Now Sally is in your network as a first-level connection, and all first-level connections can be contacted with a free, direct message. Your second-degree connections include all the people who are first-level connections with Sally. For example, if Sally worked with John at another company and they are first level connections, now John is your second-level connection. You can ask Sally for an introduction to John and send John an invitation to connect; if he accepts, he becomes a first-level connection with you.

Let's say that you haven't yet invited John into your network. Sally is a first-level connection; John is a second-level connection. Your third-level connections are all the first-level connections of John, your second-level connection. Say you wanted to meet Mike, a third-level connection who is connected on a first level with John. The process is that you would send an introduction request through Sally to John to meet his connection, Mike. You create a message asking Sally to send it to John to send it on to Mike. In most cases, your first-level connection, Sally, will be happy to forward the introduction request on to John and Mike.

Why is that? It's primarily because LinkedIn exists entirely for networking. People understand why you are there and will most often send on your requests. From personal experience, I know that I send on 100 percent of the introduction requests I get. I feel fine doing it because I know that the person getting the request has the complete right to accept it or ignore it. It's really up to the other person if he or she wants to make the connection. So I and many others forward all requests. Now, as you will learn later, there are many communication methods available to you on LinkedIn for you to reach other professionals with whom you are not first-level connections.

* * *

Now you know the basic rules for marketing yourself on LinkedIn and how the site is structured. The sky's the limit. This is your opportunity to use the world's largest professional network. Starting with the next chapter, you will learn how to build your foundation for success on LinkedIn: a powerful, user-friendly, and customer-focused profile.

Chapter 2: The LinkedIn Profile: Your Miniwebsite

Creating a Powerful Profile

If you are like many people, you've gotten an invitation to connect on LinkedIn. If you don't have an account yet, simply go to www.linkedin.com and sign up for an account. All you need to do is enter your name, email address, and a password. LinkedIn will send you a confirmation email, and you click it to confirm that this is indeed your email account. Then log into LinkedIn using your email address and password, and you are ready to go.

You might be tempted to start looking for contacts to invite as connections, but hold off on that just for a little while. You have a different goal at first, and that is 100 percent completeness of your LinkedIn profile. LinkedIn even has a measuring tool that shows how far you have come in creating a complete profile. On the right side of your screen, you'll see a box that displays your profile completeness, and you'll see that it's at 25 percent just for signing up for an account. Congratulations! The next step is to get to 100 percent complete, which brings with it many benefits. This includes showing up in more searches for your expertise, and showing the world that you are taking your networking on LinkedIn seriously—and people should take you seriously as well.

To get to 100 percent, you need to add the following:

- A current position with description
- Industry and postal code
- Two more positions
- Education
- At least 5 skills
- Profile photo
- At least 50 connections
- A summary

When you complete these basics, you can start to add some connections, but you will never really be done with your profile. Your profile is your "miniwebsite" on LinkedIn that you can constantly modify with your latest achievements and with content that separates you from the crowd and demonstrates your expertise. It's where everyone will come to once they have "met" you in other areas of LinkedIn, such as Groups or Answers, and where you want to impress them! So work on your profile every day to make sure it does the best job of representing who you are and what you can offer.

I recommend you spend a lot of time creating a fantastic profile. Yes, you do need to spend time networking in the various functions of LinkedIn, but remember that it's your profile where people you want to impress will ultimately end up once you meet them. Since your profile is so important, we are going to spend the next several chapters on creating a world-class profile. Let's start with the basics.

How to Make Your Profile Rock!

Your home base on LinkedIn is your profile. It's where everyone goes to see who you are once they've seen your LinkedIn Groups posts, enlightening answers in LinkedIn Answers, or status update where you posted an intriguing question. Don't confuse your profile with a résumé because it needs to be so much more. It's actually a miniwebsite that you can customize to create a multidimensional marketing tool for yourself, either as a service provider, a job seeker, an entrepreneur seeking funding, or whatever your current status is.

First of all, in everything you do on your profile, make sure it is client- and user-focused. When you first meet a prospective client, you don't rattle off all your accomplishments that you've memorized by rote; you don't blurt out where you worked and how amazing you are; you don't whip out your diploma.

No, the first thing you do is figure out how you can help that client, what problems you can solve, and what results you can help him or her achieve. Since LinkedIn is for making connections—and for the majority of professionals, that means clients and business partners—you need to design your profile to create that "client-focused," benefit-oriented approach. Your profile should answer the question, "What's in it for me, your potential client or partner?" So focus on the benefits you will provide and how you will provide them.

Another thing to keep in mind is that we have become a race of time-pressed, multitasking, instant-gratification-seeking humans. We have drive-through coffee stands, banks, pharmacies, and even weddings (in Vegas); movies on demand on every device imaginable; and QR (quick response) codes on every item in the department store so we can pull up instant data and reviews. And when it comes to reading, we are all scanners. We want the pertinent facts fast and without a lot of work. We want easily digestible bites of information. We prefer *Dilbert* over *War and Peace*.

That means your profile should be scannable by someone in a hurry (which is all of us). Avoid big blocks of text. Get in and get out, and your reader will thank you.

Designing the Perfect Information Box

On your profile, the first thing people read is the large box on the top of the page with a slight gray background. Let's first work on that to make sure your first impression is a perfect one.

Use a Professional Photograph

LinkedIn is all about people connecting with people, and we do business with those we know, like, and trust. Here you want a professional headshot, and a nice pleasant smile goes a long way toward making your profile inviting to read. Avoid the cutesy route that works okay on Facebook where you show your Labrador or your cute three-year-old child; stay away from pictures of two people (it's nice that you have a significant other, but this profile is about you); and don't use a cartoon or something silly. And even though quick response codes are all the rage, avoid the temptation and show us your smiling face.

To add a photo, click on *Profile > Edit Profile*. Click on *Edit Photo* in the photo space and upload a photo from your computer.

Create a Great Professional Headline

When people find you in searches on LinkedIn, read your discussion posts in Groups, or see what you've written in LinkedIn Answers, they see a little box with your name, photo, and headline.

Don't be like most people who have the default setting where LinkedIn just takes your current job title and makes it your headline. Boring! This does not give people a clue as to why they should connect with you or do business with you, or how you can help them.

Make it a benefit-oriented headline. Show what you can do to help people. There are two ways to do that. One, if you have several different skills, list them as words, capitalize each word, and separate them with a straight up-and-down line—it looks neater than dots or asterisks. (You make the line by holding down the shift key and the "\".) Here is how I have my headline:

Dan Sherman
LinkedIn Expert® I Social Media Trainer I Coach I Speaker I
Author I Internet Marketer I 16,000+ Connections

Another approach to your professional headline is the "benefit statement" approach. This is when you put into a sentence how you can help people, especially if you are only focused on one area of expertise, for example:

Top Graphic Designer Makes All Your Promotional Materials Pull Customers In Like a Magnet
Expert Webmaster Creates Sites That Engage, Enlighten, and Convert Your Prospects into Raving Fans

If your target market is localized, then make your headline localized as well. Get specific; think niche, such as:

Helping Small Businesses in Boise Get the Most from Their IT Investment
Assisting Home Buyers in Orlando to Find Their Dream Home Fast and Efficiently

You get the idea. Turn yourself into a direct response copywriter when writing your headline, and tell the world what benefits you offer. One strategy you can use is to look at the profiles of other professionals who do what you do and see what they have put in their headline. If you see something great, follow their lead. Make your headline concise, compelling, and value-driven and you'll stand out from those who just use the default first job title.

To change your headline, go to the top menu bar, click on *Profile > Edit Profile,* click *Edit* by your name, then under Basic Information fill in a new headline in the Headline section (see Figure 2-1).

Website Section

Here is another place where you can customize your profile to make it benefit-oriented. You can list three websites here, and LinkedIn gives you the choice of standard names for the sites in the drop-down, such as "My company" or "My blog." At the bottom of the drop-down is "other." What you want to do is select "other" and then put in some kind of benefit-oriented statement.

11

Figure 2-1. In the Basic Information section, you have the opportunity to write a professional headline that describes the benefit you offer to anyone wishing to do business with you.

Make it a call to action by offering something in the name of the site that gives people a reason to go there! You can use "Download a free real estate report," "Get a lead generating system," or "View 10 Free Social Media Videos." By using something catchy, you will get more people to the site you want them to visit, where they can connect with you, join your mailing list (and get into your sales funnel), sign up for a free 30-minute consultation—whatever is the next logical step for your prospects. Job seekers can send readers of their profile who click on a website link to an online portfolio or any site where their work and expertise is on display. Entrepreneurs can direct potential investors to a site with their start-up information and goals.

Here is what I am using in my website section:

- Free Social Media Tips: takes readers to my main site, where they can learn about social media and sign up for my seminars
- Learn Social Media Strategies: leads people to my online course on social media marketing, where they can purchase an online home study course

- LinkedIn Classes in Florida: takes you to an invitation from Eventbrite (a great web-based site where you can create events and it collects the payment for you), where you can sign up for LinkedIn classes.

To change your website descriptions, click on *Profile > Edit Profile*. Then click on *Edit Contact Info* by the small Rolodex card image. Click *Edit* next to each website; choose *Other* in the drop-down menu, and add your call to action; and remember to click on *Save Changes* and test your links! (See Fig 2-2.) To test them, go to *Profile > View Profile*, look at your profile as if you were a first-time visitor, and try the links out to make sure you entered the URL correctly. (Don't forget the http. You might want to copy and paste the URL right from the top address bar on the site.)

Figure 2-2. To create interesting descriptions for the websites listed in your main information box, click *Edit* next to Websites and then on the Edit screen select *Other* from the drop-down menu and add a descriptive term.

Twitter

If you have a Twitter account, add it here under the Website section. Click on *Edit* next to Twitter, and you will get a box where you can add your Twitter account and manage your Twitter settings.

Customize Your Profile Link

When you first sign up for LinkedIn and get your profile, your public link that you use to send traffic to your profile will be cluttered. It will say something like "linkedin.com/ins/ joesmith49393." You'll want to clean it up and make it simple by changing it to just your first and last name. Then you can put it on your business cards, in your email signature, on your website, on other social sites... anywhere you want in order to drive traffic to your profile. Once you see how robust you can make your profile, you might even decide you don't need a website; you can drive all your traffic to it.

If the name you want is taken, try adding a middle initial or different variations of your name. Another approach, which I use and many people have also used, is to turn your public profile link into a personal branding URL, a tag line that shows people what you can do for them. Examples would be:

linkedin.com/in/atlantaplumber
linkedin.com/in/greenthumb
linkedin.com/in/expertcoder
linkedin.com/in/orlandorealtor
linkedin.com/in/linkedinspeaker (this is the one I use)

You don't get many characters—just enough to be creative. Make something you will want to put everywhere.

To change your public profile URL and adjust your public profile settings, click on *Profile > Edit Profile*. Next to the small LinkedIn "in" logo and your existing URL, click *Edit*. This takes you to a page where you can customize how your LinkedIn profile looks when someone finds it in the search engines.

You can check and uncheck boxes for what you want displayed. On the right side, you will see *Customize Your Public Profile*. There is where you can select what you want the public to see. I have everything checked because I want everything to show, but you can customize yours. In the lower right of this page, you will see *Your Public Profile URL*. Click on *Customize your public profile URL*.

You will then get a box where you can put what you want after the "linkedin.com/in" in your public URL, then click on *Set Custom URL* (see Figure 2-3).

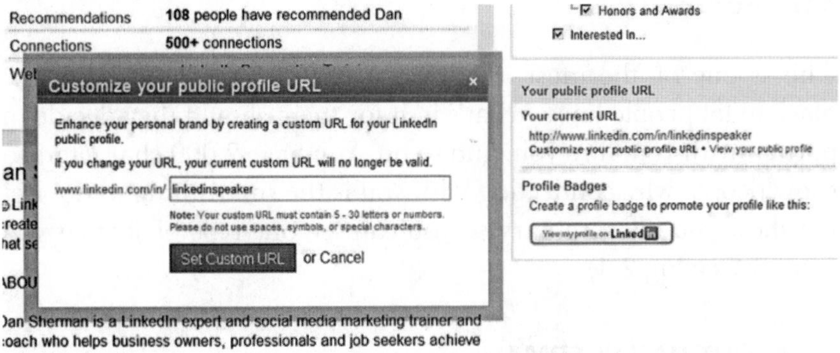

Figure 2-3. You can customize your public profile URL with your name or a branding term to create a short and memorable web address to use for directing people to your LinkedIn profile.

Lastly, on the bottom of the Information box, you will see a blue button that says *View profile*, which takes you to the view of your profile that everyone on LinkedIn sees. On the right side of this button is a drop-down arrow that, when you press it, reveals four options: *Ask for a recommendation* takes you to the page where you can request recommendations from your first-level connections; *Create profile in another language* allows you to create a profile in over 40 languages; *Share* gives you several options for sharing your LinkedIn profile on the web; and *Export to PDF* instantly gives you a copy of your profile in a PDF format.

Creating the Ad for You, Inc.

Now that we've finished with the Information box, there is much more to do to make your profile a complete advertisement for the brand known as You, Inc. The following are all parts of your profile that you can customize. You can then arrange them in any order simply by hovering your mouse over the title of the section, waiting until you see the four arrows or crosshairs symbol, and dragging sections to wherever you want in your profile.

Your Summary

This is one of the most important parts of your profile. It's the place to let people know what's in it for them should they decide to partner with you, hire you, and so on. You have 2,000 characters to show people why connecting with you is the smart thing to do. Let me show you my summary so you can see one type of format you can use (see Fig 2-4).

ABOUT DAN SHERMAN
Dan Sherman is a LinkedIn expert and social media marketing trainer and coach who helps business owners and professionals achieve new levels of success. He leverages his 20+ years of corporate marketing experience, sales training

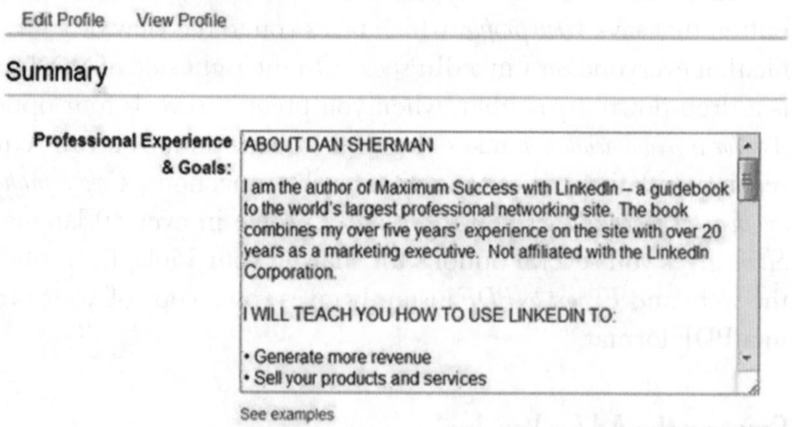

Edit Profile   View Profile

Summary

Professional Experience & Goals:
ABOUT DAN SHERMAN

I am the author of Maximum Success with LinkedIn – a guidebook to the world's largest professional networking site. The book combines my over five years' experience on the site with over 20 years as a marketing executive. Not affiliated with the LinkedIn Corporation.

I WILL TEACH YOU HOW TO USE LINKEDIN TO:

• Generate more revenue
• Sell your products and services

See examples

Figure 2-4 On the Summary Page in Edit Profile mode, you have the opportunity to write a compelling ad for yourself describing in detail who you are and what kind of value you can provide to other LinkedIn members.

background, six years on LinkedIn, and his passion for Internet marketing to help professionals achieve their goals and objectives with LinkedIn.

DAN CAN TEACH YOU HOW TO USE LINKEDIN TO:
- Generate more revenue
- Sell your products and services
- Generate unlimited quality leads
- Find the right employees and partners
- Drive hordes of traffic to your website
- Build your contact and prospect lists
- Become a thought leader and expert in your field
- Find lucrative consulting, freelance, and full-time work

LEARN MORE ABOUT DAN'S WORK HERE:
- Download articles and the brochure from "Dan Sherman's Files"
- Explore his courses, articles, and books in "Publications"

LEARN LINKEDIN FROM A LINKEDIN EXPERT:
- Public seminars and online trainings
- One-on-one consultations
- Training programs at your company

INVITE DAN TO TEACH:
- Get LinkedIn to Profits
- Social Media Marketing to Grow Your Business
- Build Your Personal Brand with LinkedIn
- Turn Your Passion into Profits
- Internet Marketing Strategies for Entrepreneurs
- Beginner, Intermediate, and Advanced LinkedIn Workshops

DAN'S PHILOSOPHY
LinkedIn is the most powerful resource you can use to build any kind of business or career you desire, and Dan can show you how to use LinkedIn to its full capabilities.

Dan Sherman is an open networker and accepts all LinkedIn invitations.

Connect with me on LinkedIn using:

danontheweb@live.com

Join "Link Success With Dan Sherman"—Dan's LinkedIn Group

Need a speaker for your group on LinkedIn and social media marketing? Call LinkedIn Expert Dan Sherman.

The Reasons Behind My Format Choice

Since we are all scanners, I believe the summary should be easy to scan. That's why I chose the outline format: because it's easy to read quickly, and it's what I recommend you do. Essentially, in your summary, you should tell people:

1. Who you are
2. Who you help
3. How you can help them
4. How to get in touch with you

Start off with a few sentences that describe who you are and sum up your professional qualifications. Then use the headline and bullet format as I have done. You will see that I introduce myself, then I go right into what I can do for you, how I will do it, and in what modes I can help you. I also clearly point out what I can speak about should you desire to hire me. Everything is neat, concise, and to the point, and it can be easily consumed.

I also use the summary to alert my reader to some of the multimedia aspects and resources I have in my LinkedIn profile where they can learn more about me, such as my brochure and my list of publications. No one is a mind reader. If you want your potential clients and partners to get the full picture of what you offer, show them where to look in your profile. I also advertise one of my LinkedIn groups where people can join and share ideas on how to get the most from LinkedIn. This encourages more people to join my group, thus expanding my sphere of influence.

You'll see that I include some very important contact information in my summary. I am a LinkedIn Open Networker (which you will sometimes see abbreviated as LION), which means I want to grow my network as big as I can to give me as much exposure as possible to potential opportunities for consulting, speaking, the media, partners, and so on. That's why I include the statement that I accept all invitations and I give my email address to make it easy to invite me to connect.

Open Versus Closed Networkers

Let me clarify: some people who use LinkedIn restrict themselves to connecting only with people they know. For me, that doesn't work. I want as big a network as possible, since I don't know who knows someone who knows someone who can give me my next big opportunity. LinkedIn says to connect only with people you know, so if too many people click on the *Report Spam* button when you send them an invitation, it will penalize you and put restrictions on your account.

That's why I tell people I will never report them. I want invitations from everyone to grow my network, and I assure them that I will accept all invitations. (Maybe one in a hundred I don't accept because they have a goofy cartoon for a picture or a headline that seems like it's a fake profile or a "phishing" scam. In that case, I just click on the *Ignore* button and move on without hitting *Report Spam*.)

Include Your "Call to Action"

Also, in your summary, remember to include a call to action. Your summary states what you can do for them; now don't make them hunt for a way to contact you and pay you lots of money. As the movie title said, *It's all about the Benjamins!* Include your phone number or email address—however you want to be contacted. For example, when you go to my LinkedIn profile, you'll see that I include my phone number. As a speaker, I want to make it easy for people to call me. Do whatever you are comfortable doing, but in all cases make it easy for people to do business with you by giving them lots of contact points.

Promoting More than One Kind of Expertise

What if you have several kinds of businesses and you help people in many ways? You can try a variation of the summary outline I've suggested by having blocks of information that reference each of your skill areas.

For example, let's say you have three skills. You are a graphic designer, website builder, and copywriter. (Hey, you're pretty talented—we should talk!) I recommend you start with an overall statement, such as:

Who I Am
Joe Smith is a talented communications professional
with many years of experience helping business owners
generate more sales and profits with superior branding and
promotional materials.

Then you would have a section for each skill, noting who you help and how you help them:

Graphic Designer
Who I Help
I help small businesses with their graphic needs, etc.
How I Work with You
I can design your business cards, letterhead, etc.

and so on for each of your three skills. You are limited in the summary to 2,000 characters, so if you put multiple skills and companies in there, you will have to keep each one short and punchy. If there is a specific place where you want readers to go to learn more about each skill set, then put a call to action in each area. So, in the previous example, if you have a site just for graphic design, include a call to action with a URL just for that one area. (There is no place to put a hyperlink in the summary, but there are many places to do so in the rest of the profile.) Do the same for each of your "skill blocks."

Some final thoughts on the summary. As you spend time on LinkedIn, you will see profile summaries that are simply people boasting about how great they are and what they've achieved. No one cares except a mom. Tell people what you can do for them. As we say in sales, your customers are tuned to one station: WII-FM (what's in it for me). *CREATIVE SOLUTIONS TO THE MOST DEMANDING DESIGN (BRAND ENHANCED)*

Second, I don't expect you to have a complete *Webster's Dictionary* in your brain. That's what spell-check is for. So write your summary in a word processing program, spell-check it, then copy and paste it into LinkedIn. That way your spelling is accurate and you can pull symbols in (like the bullets I got from MS Word; there are other symbols you can use if you like—I've seen musicians use the notes icon). Remember: you get only one chance to make a good first impression! A profile with lots of typos will most likely defeat any purpose you have on LinkedIn, no matter what you are trying to achieve.

Fill Out Your Work Experience

Did you ever go into a job interview, and the interviewer said something like, "So, tell me about yourself"?

One of the first things LinkedIn will ask you to do is fill out your work experiences. In this section you have the opportunity to tell potential clients, partners, hiring managers, and investors what you're all about and what you've been up to all these years. If you're just out of college, even though you don't have a lot of experience, there are plenty of options for information to put here. You see, they don't have to be nine-to-five jobs; they just need to be positions or activities where you obtained experience relatable to the work world. For those of us more "seasoned" (I love that term—it makes us sound like lamb chops, right?), there's lots to talk about. For our experience section, we can relate the journey we have been on, or, as the Grateful Dead said, "What a long, strange trip it's been."

One question is, do you mention every place you have ever worked? The answer is for the most part "yes," and there are good reasons why, as you'll soon learn. However, you should exclude jobs that really do not contribute to your professional career, make it easier for people to find you, or add to your credibility—like the summer you spent fitting people with penny loafers in a shoe store, or getting a tan as a lifeguard, or manning a Tilt-a-Wheel at the Jersey shore. Those jobs you can leave off because they don't make you more desirable as a service provider or more employable, and no one from those jobs will be looking to connect with you.

Other than jobs that don't elevate your professional status, put every decent company you have ever worked for on your profile. Adding a great company, even though you were on a lower level or even an intern, adds credibility to your profile. You're associating with a great brand name, and it gives other people who worked there and are looking at your profile a personal connection with you and a reason to trust and like you. You've got something in common.

Another reason to list all your relevant jobs is that recommendations must be associated with a position you listed in Experience. You can't have a general recommendation that says something like, "She's an all-around great person." Recommendations are crucial to building your brand on LinkedIn, and they are social proof that you are the wonder kid you say you are. Every position you list gives you another opportunity to include a rousing recommendation from a colleague, boss, satisfied client, business partner, and so on.

Adding Non-Full-Time Jobs

You can and should include volunteer positions, as it gives viewers of your profile a chance to see that you are giving back to your community and you're a well-rounded individual. For new graduates with very little job experience, posting volunteer jobs shows that you have been actively involved in different industries, that you were a team player, and perhaps that you held some leadership roles.

Listing and describing volunteer jobs is also handy when you are filling out your profile should you currently be unemployed and looking for work. Saying that you are president, membership chairman, or volunteer coordinator of a local charity as your *Current Position* tells hiring managers you're not sitting on your sofa eating Oreos and watching *Mad Men*. You're active in the community and polishing your people skills. Another great option for this same situation is to start a LinkedIn Group, and list your current role as "Group Manager, ABC LinkedIn Group." It shows that you are not only active and social media savvy, but also a thought leader in your field.

Take some time crafting the job description; don't be tempted to put in just your titles and leave it at that. You never know which accomplishment of yours will be the one that puts you ahead of the competition in the eyes of a potential client or employer. Fill your descriptions with keywords, the skills and job titles that people will be searching on in LinkedIn to get the expertise they need. If you know a certain programming language or you're an expert in a graphic design program, put it in. Use care crafting the description, since it tells the story of who you are as a professional and gives you the chance to use lots of keywords. (Keywords are the terms that people search on in LinkedIn when looking for experts.)

Even part-time work can be listed in your Experience section, especially if it has to do with what you want to be branded for, since you can use a lot of keywords in the job description. For example, I want to be branded as a LinkedIn expert. So, in my profile, I list several consulting assignments in my Experience section where I was a LinkedIn trainer at different corporations and professional groups. Since that term is what I want to be branded as and found for, I include several of these, even though they were short-term positions.

Arranging the Order of Jobs

Go to *Profile > Edit Profile*. Find the Experience section and click on the *+ Add a position* link on the right. A box will come up where you put your company name, title, location, time period, and description. If this is a position you currently hold, click the box that says *I currently work here*.

Basically, if you click the box near the position saying "I work here," it shows up near the top of your Experience section, and if you don't, it shows up lower. For keyword optimization, you want several job titles in positions you hold now and those in the past to include keywords that you want to be found for. To add your past jobs, click on + *Add a position,* don't click the *I currently work here* box, and put in the start and end months and years you worked there. If you are unemployed and searching, it's okay to leave your current job in the Experience section as long as you add an end date to the job to alert recruiters and hiring managers that you are available.

To change the order of the jobs that you currently hold (for example, let's say you list some current part-time jobs, a volunteer position, and a consulting assignment), it's easy to arrange them in the order in which you want readers to see them. In the *Edit Profile* mode, simply hover your mouse over any job where you have indicated you currently work and drag and drop it.

Adding Sections That Make Your Profile Shine

Just under the main information box, you will see a tiny hyperlink feature over to the right that says + *Add sections* where you can add areas to your profile to reflect honors, achievements, and experiences. Click on + *Add sections* to get started. You will have the opportunity to add lots of sections that you can use to really tell your story and give readers a glimpse into your professional life (see Figure 2-5). Sections you can add include:

- Certifications
- Publications
- Courses
- Honors and Awards
- Organizations
- Projects
- Patents
- Test Scores
- Volunteer Experience and Causes

Everyone has a different background, and you will add different sections that will help you tell your complete story on LinkedIn.

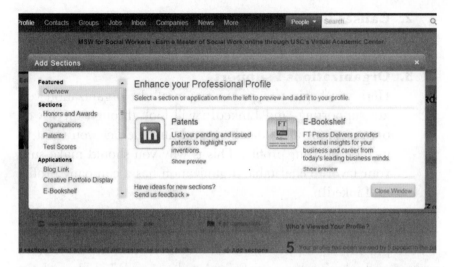

Figure 2-5. When you click on + *Add sections* under the main information box on your profile in Edit Profile mode, you will see this box displayed, which gives you several options listed on the left for you to add informative sections to your profile.

Look at the choices and see what sections you want to add that will make your profile stand out. Of the optional sections listed previously, I am using Volunteer Experience & Causes and Publications. I encourage you to add the volunteer section to your profile. After all, one of your top priorities when developing your profile should be to help the readers see you as a credible, interesting person with whom they want to do business. Showing your involvement with local and national charities tells another part of your professional story, and this may be appealing to some of the people with whom you are trying to create relationships.

The Volunteer Experience & Causes section is really three topics in one:

1. **Volunteer positions I have held**
   You can include the name of the organization, your position, time frame for your service, and a detailed description of the mission and purpose of the organization.

2. **Causes I care about**

   You can choose from a list LinkedIn provides or enter your own specific cause.

3. **Organizations I support**

   Here you begin to type the name of the organization you are supporting, and LinkedIn will look through the list of organizations in its database and find the one you want to include on your profile. This is why you should make sure your favorite charitable organization has a company profile on LinkedIn.

I also use the optional section called Publications. There is where I have put my books, my two online courses, and articles I have written and submitted to www.EzineArticles.com. What I love about this section is that the title of each item is hyperlinked and there is a space to describe the publication. So people who read about my books and want to learn more can click on the title, and away they go to Amazon.com. Those who want to buy more courses click on their titles, and off they go to the promotional pages on the web. Similarly, the EzineArticles.com titles click through to my articles on that site.

So if you have any article on the web that shows you are an expert; if you've published a story in an online magazine; if you have a book on Amazon.com; if you have an online course to sell . . . if you have literally anything written on the web that you want people to have instant access to, add the Publications section and link to it. It will give your profile depth, add to your branding as an expert, and give you the chance to add unlimited URLs to your profile. Just click on *+ Add a Publication* in this section, add the title and the corresponding URL, and describe what people are going to read.

What if you have a white paper on your site that you want people to read? First, add the Publications section to your profile by clicking on *Profile > Edit Profile*, clicking on *+ Add sections*, and adding that section. Then add your website URL and a description of the publication users are going to find on your site.

Another great section to add is the Projects section. Like the Publications section, it offers you the chance to add unlimited URLs to your profile. For example, I worked with a client recently who had a construction company, and he really wanted to highlight his company's completed projects and show them to prospects visiting his profile. So we added the Projects section, then added each project description, and hyperlinked them to photos he had previously uploaded to Flickr, a free photo-sharing site. This way his prospects could actually see the great work his firm had done. So the Projects section is a great way to provide proof in living color of what you have achieved in your career.

* * *

Now you've laid the groundwork for an amazing profile. But there's more to do. Let's continue with the next thing you must add to your profile in order to give you the advantage over your competition: social proof, or recommendations.

Chapter 3:
What Goes Around: Giving and Getting Recommendations

Your profile is your work of art, your *Mona Lisa*, your *David* statue, your Sistine Chapel ceiling. Everything on it has been placed there by you to build your brand as the go-to person in your field, the expert unequaled in the modern world.

Everything was created by you, except one important section that can help determine your success on LinkedIn: Recommendations.

Recommendations are proof that you are as good as you say you are in your profile. Fortunately, LinkedIn gives you the chance to get recommendations from a wide variety of people, so you'll never be at a loss for endorsements to add to your profile to create what has become so crucial in today's transparent Internet world—namely, social proof. You can tell people how great you are, but no one is really going to believe it until someone else (besides a close relative or your sweetheart) is there to agree.

It reminds me of the famous *New Yorker* cartoon that summed up the perils of trusting what you see online. Two dogs are in front of a computer, and one is typing away and says to the other dog: "On the Internet, no one knows you're a dog."

Put another way, on the Internet, you often don't know what you're getting. Because so many people have been burned by believing what they read online, there is now a wariness and distrust of anything on a website. In recent years the Federal Trade Commission (FTC) has jumped into the fray and created laws to protect consumers from merchants who display fake testimonials and fake blogs; however, the Internet is so vast it's impossible to police every single company.

Social proof goes a long way toward calming the fears of people. It's easy to add it to your LinkedIn profile, and it can come from a variety of places. You can ask colleagues past and present, bosses past and present, people who reported to you, business partners, professors, people who did work for you...literally anyone you participated in some kind of work with in the past. What makes recommendations great social proof that's believable is that the names of the people who recommended you show up as hyperlinks next to their recommendations, so they can be easily checked out and their praise corroborated.

Social Proof Is the Key to Success

So, why are endorsements so crucial to your success? First of all, recommendations form a key element of your profile, and the number of recommendations you have received for each position is noted under each job. When someone is choosing between two people for work or consulting, if one person has lots of strong recommendations in his or her profile, which detail specific accomplishments and goals met, while the other person has none, the hirer will probably give the person with recommendations the first shot at the opportunity. LinkedIn is all about seizing the moment, so you've got to be ready with a killer profile that includes recommendations.

I had an experience recently when I was presenting to a marketing company that was interested in hiring me for LinkedIn training, and also partnering with me as a trainer to its clients. As I spoke, I pulled up my profile on the large 50-inch plasma TV mounted on the wall, and scrolled thorough it, including my recommendations (which number around 150). The president of the company looked at it and said, "Wow. Lots of recommendations! That's good." I knew I had scored some points, and I indeed got the training job and signed that company up as a referral partner.

Second, when LinkedIn users search for certain skills, they use keywords, and the words in recommendations are "keyword searchable." That's why you might offer to help write them, as we'll see in a bit.

Third, the number of recommendations you have helps determine how high you show up in rankings when people do a LinkedIn search. Because of LinkedIn's search algorithm, all things being equal, you appear higher above other people's profiles who have the same keywords if you have more recommendations.

Preparing to Get Recommendations

Now's a good time to start thinking about all the people who can contribute a recommendation and help you with this crucial aspect of your profile on LinkedIn. But not everyone can write you a recommendation; the only ones who can do so are LinkedIn members who are directly connected to you (in other words, first-level connections). That's why it's important to connect with anyone you've ever worked with who might contribute a recommendation.

So if you know people who would write you a great recommendation, but who haven't made the plunge and established themselves on LinkedIn, you might consider sharing some of the benefits of being on the site, showing them how to sign up and connect with you, then asking for the recommendation. You'll be doing them a favor and getting some more social proof for your profile.

If someone is already on LinkedIn who you feel would give you a great recommendation, but you're not first-level connections yet, then take that step and invite that person to connect. Once you do, you can request a recommendation.

Getting Recommendations from First-Level Connections

Simply go to *Profile > Recommendations > Request Recommendations* and follow these steps.

1. **Choose what you want to be recommended for** by picking out a position from the drop-down menu (see Figure 3-1). This is why it's so important to fill out your work experience

section completely with all the positions you've held. It gives you a wider range of positions to get recommendations for—be they part time, full time, or volunteer.

2. **Decide whom you'll ask**. Click on the blue LinkedIn box on the right and a box will display with your first-level contacts. Put a check by each person's name. I recommend just asking one person at a time, even though you have the ability to "group ask" up to 200 people at once. Getting recommendations is just too important a task to create a mass mailing that might not have the same effect as a highly personalized request.

3. **Create your message**. The system provides a very vanilla, watered-down request. Erase that bad boy immediately! You are building the crucial part of your profile; don't take shortcuts by just sending what someone at LinkedIn wrote. Besides, you are asking for someone's time, so the least you can do is write a short note. Create a very specific request based on what the two of you did together, for example:

It was great working with you on the Bruce Willis "Great Moments of Sensitivity in Cinema" retrospective. Who knew there were so many? It would mean a lot to me if you could recommend my work on the project....

You get the idea. When that treasured recommendation comes back, you'll get notified in your LinkedIn inbox. At that point, you will have a few choices:

1. **Accept it.** If it was what you wanted, accept it and it goes right on your profile.
2. **Request a revision.** If it did not come out the way you wanted—for example, you wish to highlight a certain aspect of the role or work, or something was incorrect— you can send it back with a polite note asking the person to modify it and then give her some suggestions for the changes.

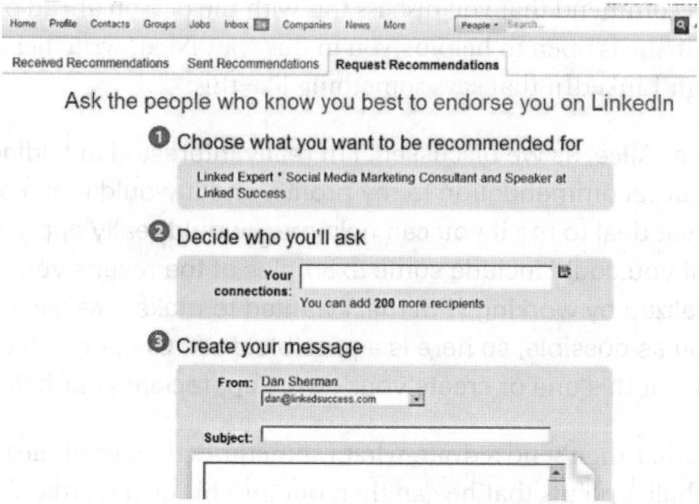

Figure 3-1. The Request Recommendation form gives you a way to add social proof to your profile by enabling you to write to your first-level connections and ask them to provide a testimonial for the work you did together. Be sure to customize the message to your connection.

3. **Hide it.** If for some reason you changed your mind and no longer want this person recommending you, or you want to downplay that position, just hide it and the world will never see it.

One way to ensure that the recommendation you get is the one you want is to provide a little assistance. You may have noticed: we're all a little busy. The person from whom you want the recommendation may have too much on his plate to sit down and play Shakespeare for you. That's okay. You can write the recommendation for him just the way you want it to appear, with all the great keywords you want to be found for, and send it to him. He can then use it all or edit it and send it back. Try this, if it fits your style. People are often glad to give you recommendations but don't have the time and are appreciative of the fact that they can recommend you without working up a sweat.

I recommend that you discuss this with the person ahead of time to see if she is open to helping you in this way. Next, write her a note through LinkedIn that says something like this:

> Dear Alice, as we discussed, I'm really interested in adding your recommendation to my profile, and it would mean a great deal to me if you can help me. I would really appreciate it if you could include some examples of the results you realized by working with me. I wanted to make it as easy on you as possible, so here is a possible draft. Of course, feel free to edit this one or create your own. I appreciate your help.

Rather then send a draft, what I sometimes do is send the person a few bullet points that he can then put into his own words. You see, he doesn't know exactly what you are trying to build your brand as; he is too busy building his! So I keep a bullet point list on my computer and send that off when someone says he will write a recommendation for me but wants to know what to say.

One thing to keep in mind when you ask for recommendations is that you're actually doing your contacts a favor when they send you one. That's because now their names show up on your profile, which gives them added exposure to your network. Since my profile is viewed quite often, I use that as a small bargaining chip when I approach contacts for a recommendation.

Want More Recommendations? Write Some!

What if you're just starting out in the working world and you don't know anyone who would recommend you? Or, what if you are just starting out on LinkedIn altogether? What's the best way to prime the pump? Start writing recommendations for anyone you can think of. Write five or ten a day and get the ball rolling!

Go through your contacts by going to *Contacts > Connections,* which will bring up your first-level contacts. Go through the list, first sorting contacts by location to find people in your area whom you know. Chances are that you worked on something together for which you can recommend them. Then make a list of anyone you worked with or had a positive experience with. (It could be a mentor, teacher, colleague, employer, vendor, customer, or someone you served with on a volunteer committee if you don't have a lot of job experience.)

Then once you know whom you want to recommend, go back to *Contacts > Connections* and open up their profile. Look for the blue *Send a message* button at the bottom of their Information box and click on the down arrow to reveal a drop-down menu. Click on *Recommend* and you'll be asked to select the category of recommendation (Colleague, Service Provider, Business partner, or fellow Student) and press *Go* and the recommendation form will display. Pick the job you are recommending that person for and your relationship with her at the time, then write a very specific recommendation that is genuine. (See Figure 3-2.)

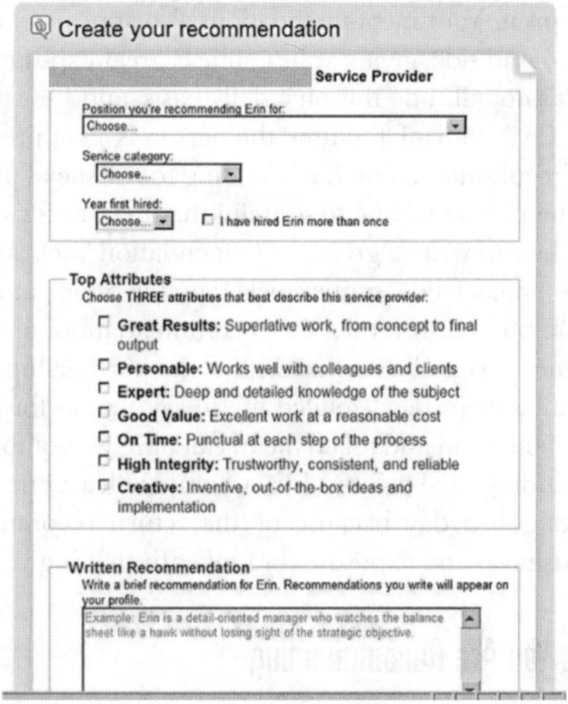

Figure 3-2. The recommendation form offers you the chance to select three attributes of the person you are recommending and then offer a sincere testimonial for his or her work. Writing unsolicited recommendations is a good idea and can lead to unexpected benefits.

Put some thought and energy into it. Begin by looking at the person's profile and checking out his professional headline and summary. You'll see just what that person is promoting as his brand and what keywords he is using to be found. Then by incorporating that into your recommendation, you can write one that the person is likely to accept and that will help optimize his profile. Another reason why it's a good idea to check the person's profile before you write is that he might have changed his career focus and desired branding since the last time you worked with him.

When you send off your unsolicited recommendation, you are going to make that person's day! Don't forget, you also benefit when he accepts it because your name is now on his profile hyperlinked back to you, and you get added exposure and potential additional traffic back to your profile. Write a great recommendation to ensure that the person accepts it. Your recommendations also appear on your profile on the right-hand side, giving your contacts great exposure.

But that's not all. I do this on a daily basis, and I see great things happening. Over half of the time the person is so appreciative that he writes a recommendation back, adding to my social proof.

Often the person will be so grateful that he asks for some words from me so he can write a great recommendation back (and I'm prepared). One time a fellow trainer picked up the phone and called me to thank me, offered to return the recommendation, and then suggested we meet up and come up with some partnership ideas. The other day another trainer emailed me to say thanks for an unsolicited recommendation and asked me to call him; we got together, and he is now sending me business. I try to write at least one unsolicited recommendation a day because of the return recommendations, potential business, and exposure on LinkedIn that it gives me.

Know Who You Are Recommending

Sooner or later you are going to get a recommendation request from someone you don't know. Recently I got a request from someone asking for a recommendation based on the fact that we were both on LinkedIn. Fail! I just ignore these. Remember, it's *your* name hyperlinked to *your* profile next to the recommendation, and thus your reputation is on the line. Guard your brand wisely on LinkedIn and give recommendations only to people you know and have had a positive experience with and who you feel can do good work for others.

Just because I'm an Open Networker does not mean I will recommend anyone. I will connect with the person...but I will recommend only people I know.

Manage Your Recommendations

You have complete control over which recommendations you show. Simply go to *Profile > Recommendations >Received Recommendations*. Click on *Manage* by any position. You will get a screen displaying all your recommendations for that position (see Figure 3-3). You can click on the box that says *show* to show or hide recommendations. Under each recommendation you will also see a hyperlink that reads *Request a new or revised recommendation from...* That link takes you back to the Request Recommendation screen, where you can send out a new request.

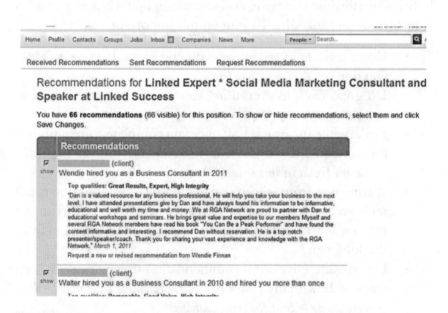

Figure 3-3. The Manage Recommendations screen gives you the opportunity to manage your recommendations for every position. You can show or hide a recommendation, request a revision, or on the bottom of the page you can see recommendations that have not been responded to and resend them.

Scroll down to the bottom of this page and you will see another section labeled *Pending recommendation requests.* Here you will see recommendation requests you made for this position that have not been answered, describing whom you wrote to and what date your request was sent. There's a hyperlink by each request that says *Resend,* which you can use to send the request again.

Everyone networks at different speeds, and everyone uses LinkedIn according to his or her own needs. I find that if a week or two has gone by after you made your request, it's okay to remind the person by resending the request from the Manage screen. Sometimes that person was too busy when the request first arrived in his or her inbox. When I resend the request, I often get the person to write me something. You have to work at it, but the effort is worth it.

Get the Social Proof You Need

I hope you see that asking for and making recommendations regularly is a worthwhile endeavor, and something that will add greatly to your success on LinkedIn. To sum up this important task:

- Don't hesitate to ask for recommendations. If you don't ask, you don't get.
- Do great work in everything you do, so everyone is glad to recommend you.
- Strike while the iron is hot; once you complete a great project for someone, ask if she will recommend you on LinkedIn while it's fresh in her mind.
- If someone from whom you want a recommendation is not tech savvy and is not on LinkedIn, make the effort to get him onboard and connected with you. He will benefit in the long run.
- Givers gain. Give out recommendations freely. You can keep track of how many you sent out by clicking on *Profile > Recommendations > Sent Recommendations.*
- Lots of quality recommendations in your profile separate you from the pack and give you credibility. Make it a part of your daily routine to give them and ask for them.

- Seek out recommendations for school, nonprofit, and volunteer work if you are just starting out in the work world.

* * *

That's it for this crucial part of your profile. Definitely add beefing up the Recommendations section of your profile to your daily list of LinkedIn tasks. Now let's really spiff up your miniwebsite on LinkedIn with a full range of free applications that will turn your profile into a 24/7 multimedia broadcasting tool for the brand of You, Inc.

Chapter 4: It's Showtime! Adding Applications for a Multimedia Profile

"There's No Business Like Show Business" is the title of a song and movie from the 1950s that celebrates the excitement and glamour of a life in show business. I agree that there's nothing like show business, and when it comes to your LinkedIn profile, there is a way to add some excitement and glamour without even taking a Greyhound to Hollywood. You will find all the pizzazz you need in LinkedIn applications.

LinkedIn provides you with a whole range of free applications that bring your profile to life, transforming it from a dry, dull, résumé-like recitation of your experiences into a multimedia extravaganza. Why be boring and one-dimensional when you can put on a show?

To start the transformation of your profile from dull to dazzling, go to *More* across the top menu, click on *Get More Applications...* , and you'll be taken to a page with all kinds of great free apps that will turn your profile into a multimedia wonderland (see Figure 4-1). The great part about adding them to your profile is that these applications are working for you 24/7 while you are busy doing other things, spreading your articles, videos, and presentations to everyone who wants to know more about you.

Let's go through the apps one by one, starting with my favorites. It will really open your eyes to how you can make your profile one of a kind to reflect the fact that you are, well, one of a kind!

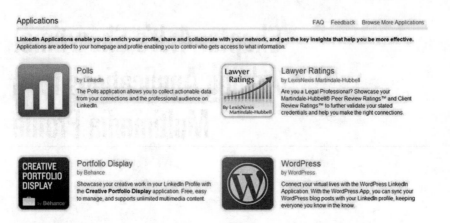

Figure 4-1. The free applications on LinkedIn give you the opportunity to add multimedia elements and extraordinary depth to your profile. They allow you to create a miniwebsite and truly stand out from the crowd.

Blogs

If you have a blog, use the Blog Link or WordPress application. Download the application, insert your URL, and every time you update your blog, a new post will appear in your profile. That way, your profile becomes a living thing that stays constantly fresh. If you want to be seen as an expert, there's no better way to continually be expressing your ideas and opinions to the professionals on LinkedIn.

The blog application also works as a traffic generator, because when people click on a post in your profile, it opens your blog in a new window. Once there, they can look around your blog and join your mailing list, view products you have for sale, find out about events you are organizing, and interact with you in a variety of ways that deepen your connection and could lead to selling more of your products and services.

SlideShare

This great application enables you to share all kinds of presentations with your profile readers. When you download it to your profile, you can add documents, portfolios, audio, videos, PDFs, and more. You can create your own automatic webinar, if you want.

I use SlideShare on my profile to play videos of testimonials from business owners who have taken my classes on how to use social media to increase their sales and profits. The videos serve several purposes for me. First, they provide more social proof for me as someone who can help people achieve success through the use of social media. Second, I put the URL of my social media online course as a footer running through one of the videos so that people can go to that site, look at my product, and purchase it.

Be creative with this application. If you don't want to put up testimonials, then put up a video of you talking about your area of expertise. Set up a small camcorder and record yourself, or have a friend interview you while filming you.

A video is great if you are a consultant or entrepreneur—you can create a 60-second commercial for yourself that tells people who you are, who you help, and how you help them in the first 30 seconds. In the next 30 seconds, you could explain how to reach you and connect with you to see if there is a possibility of working together. A video will bring your profile to life, add that show business spark, and allow your personality to shine through. It's back to the old adage: people do business with those they know, like, and trust. A video is a great start in allowing people to know the real you.

If you are a job hunter, you'll want to create a video résumé and really stand out from everyone else looking for the same position as you. Talk about what you are looking for, what you bring to the table, and how you could benefit any organization that hires you.

If you are a company owner, show off your facility with a guided tour, demonstrate how you make your product, or introduce your employees and let them talk about the products. The ways in which to use this app are endless and are bounded only by your imagination.

Here are instructions for uploading a video to SlideShare:

1. Go to More > *Get More Applications* and download the Slide-Share app to your profile.
2. Go to *Profile* > *Edit profile.*
3. Click on the SlideShare logo in the application.
4. Create a SlideShare PRO paid account and link it to your LinkedIn profile. PRO accounts start at $19/month.
5. Once you have an account, click on the *Upload* button on the top of the home page.
6. Select the video you want to upload.
7. Add a Title, Tags, Category, and Description.
8. After uploading, click on the *Publish* button.
9. Click the *Show on your profile* button on the right-hand side.

Box.net

This application lets you place several documents and MP3s on your profile that your readers can download. It's like a round-the-clock fulfillment center for You, Inc. Download the app, load it up with your documents and files, and it provides your profile viewers with readily available information.

What can you put on Box.net? Be creative!

- If you're job hunting, turn your résumé into a PDF and make it available (erasing any information you don't want on the Internet first). You can also include testimonial letters from those not on LinkedIn. If you can't get people to join and write a testimonial for your profile, turn their letters into PDFs and add them to Box.net.
- If you're a consultant, upload a PowerPoint about your company or a company brochure. I currently have my company brochure in Box.net, and I never have to mail it out anymore. I just tell prospects to visit my LinkedIn profile and download it, and as a bonus, Box.net emails me whenever someone has

downloaded my brochure. (You don't see the person's name, just that someone got a copy of your brochure.)

- If you own a company, put up pictures of your products, articles, white papers, customer testimonials... anything that helps your credibility.
- If you're launching a start-up, put up an overview of your project to get angel investors, venture capitalists, potential employees, and customers salivating about your venture.

Box.net lets you share your information with LinkedIn users, and it can provide proof of your experience and knowledge. What I mean by this is that you're an expert. You know more about something than your profile viewers—whether it's real estate lending or cost accounting or project management. So you can write tips like "10 Money-Saving Tips You Must Know When Purchasing a Phone System" or something similar, turn the list into a PDF, and let people get it from your profile. That way you are creating value first, before others meet you, thereby building a favorable impression with those with whom you want to do business.

My Box.net application is filled with articles I've written on how to succeed with LinkedIn. I get notices every day that people are downloading these LinkedIn articles from my profile, meaning that I'm advertising all the time while I'm busy doing something else. I've made sure to add my picture, email address, phone number, and website information to every PDF document I load on Box.net so that people can reach me once they read my free tips.

Here are instructions for using Box.net:

1. Go to *More > Get More Applications* and select Box.net.
2. Download the application to your profile.
3. Go to *Profile > Edit Profile,* click on Box.net, and open up a free account with them right from your profile.
4. In the *Edit Profile* mode, click on the blue menu box within the application on your profile to open up a drop-down menu.

5. Click on *Upload* from the menu, and a window will appear in which you select files from your hard drive to add to your Box.net app on your profile.

Reading List by Amazon

By downloading this application, you can share the books you are reading with your network. It's a great way to show that you are deeply involved in your subject matter and keeping up to date. In addition to allowing other people to see what you are reading and your opinions of those books, the application allows you to follow other people's reading lists.

Every time you post a book review, LinkedIn sends out a notice to your first-degree connections, which gives you more top-of-mind awareness with others and further helps you create your brand. LinkedIn will display the last two books you reviewed on your site, so think carefully about which books you display. They become part of your profile and your "real estate" on LinkedIn, and as a result become part of the brand you are creating. For example, you may wish to display two important books in your field.

For those of us with books for sale on Amazon, it's a free public-ity tool. I have in my reading list application two amazing books. One is called *You Can Be a Peak Performer!,* written by this incredible business coach who is also quite handsome... okay, you got me; it's my book. By using this application, I get to put a picture of the book cover in my profile like a mini-advertisement along with my hum-ble opinion on why everyone should read my book! I also show this book, *Maximum Success with LinkedIn,* which helps me brand myself as a LinkedIn expert. (Remember: everything you do on LinkedIn adds to your brand.)

Not only does this give me branding and advertising, but it makes buying my books a breeze. When someone clicks on my books in the Amazon application on my profile, it takes her right to the Amazon .com page, where she can enter her credit card and take advantage of Amazon's speedy delivery service.

To add books to your profile, follow these steps:

1. Go to *More > Get More Applications.*
2. Download the Reading List by Amazon app.
3. Go to *Profile > Edit Profile* and find the Amazon app.
4. Click on the *Update Your List* button. Under the line *What are you reading?*, type in the books you want to display, and Amazon will search for them in its inventory.
5. When you locate the book you want, select it, write in your review, and hit *Save.* The book will now be on your profile.

Events

This is another application I have on my profile. It's a great way to publicize my events to my connections and the entire LinkedIn network. Whenever I'm holding a LinkedIn training session, I create a LinkedIn event, and it appears on my profile and the profiles of my network.

The Events section on my profile also adds to my "findability" in LinkedIn Searches, since it is completely searchable by keywords in the event description, tags that I define, and titles of people who should consider attending. It's another way to make yourself found on LinkedIn.

Polls

Since social media is all about starting and joining conversations, the Polls feature is a really easy way to get opinions on any subject from your network and establish yourself as a thought leader. It's a great way to get your name out there and create more reasons for people to visit your profile and connect with you (which grows your network) or offer you opportunities. What's more, LinkedIn has made it easy for you to share the poll on other social networks, giving you even more visibility.

Go to *More* > *Get More Applications* > *Polls* and pull up the Polls home page. There you will be able to ask a question and specify up to five answer choices. You can then select boxes to share it on LinkedIn (such as in your status update and in up to 50 groups you belong to), your Facebook wall, and Twitter. You can also get a link to put on your blog or email signature and snag some HTML code to put it on your website. Polls are fast and easy to create, and are one more way to get your name known and give you more visibility.

Jazz Up Your Profile with Cool Applications

There are more applications that can make your profile a more rounded expression of who you are and a richer experience for your users. Take a look at each one and add the applications that create the most value for you.

Other applications you can add to your profile include:

E-Bookshelf. Read quick, concise business and career lessons from the top experts.

My Travel by TripIt. See where your LinkedIn network is traveling and when you will be in the same city as your colleagues.

Real Estate Pro. Track new property listings and available spaces and stay informed of completed deals in your area.

Legal Updates. Get legal news that matters to you and your business.

Lawyer Ratings. If you are a legal professional, you can showcase your Martindale-Hubbell Peer Review Ratings and Client Review Ratings to validate your credentials.

Portfolio Display. Showcase your creative work in your LinkedIn Profile with this app that supports unlimited multimedia content.

* * *

Take a look at all these free applications and see what you can add to your profile to increase your value to your viewers, your marketability, and your credibility. In the online world, content is king. What kind of content can you offer your readers that can help solidify your brand and establish you as an expert? Look through your articles and presentations, and then turn your profile into a miniwebsite that promotes You, Inc. Now let's look at even more sections you can add to your profile to truly set you apart from the competition.

Chapter 5: The Finishing Touches: Creating a Rocking Profile

At this point, we're almost done adding the sections that make up a world-class profile. Here are some additional important areas for you to fill out to make your profile the best it can be.

Skills & Expertise

There is a section called Skills & Expertise where you can list a whole range of your abilities. Go to *Profile > Edit Profile*, look for *Skills & Expertise,* and click on *+ Add a skill.* Start typing a skill and LinkedIn will suggest a skill from a drop-down menu. If it does not suggest a skill, that's okay; just add the skill you want to display. For example, I have many LinkedIn skills that include LinkedIn Group Management. That was not in the suggested skills, so I added it myself.

Listing your various skills is another way to demonstrate your value to potential partners and clients, so make sure you add as many as you can. Also remember that everything on your profile contributes to your being found in LinkedIn searches. When you add skills with your keywords, you increase your chances of being on top when people search for your expertise.

Another way to add skills to your profile is through the Skills & Expertise page (see Figure 5-1). On the top menu, go to *More > Skills & Expertise* and you'll be on the Skills & Expertise home page. You'll see an empty text box where you can type in one of your skills, then hit the blue *Search* button.

That will take you to the page expressly for that particular skill, giving you a viewpoint of all of LinkedIn concentrating on that one area of expertise. You will see:

- A blue button saying *Add Skill* that you can select to add it directly to the Skills & Expertise section of your profile
- A list of related skills on the left that you can consider adding right to your profile
- A definition of the skill in the center of the page
- A list of profiles of your connections who display that particular skill
- Groups devoted to that skill that you can join right from the page
- Companies that are related to that skill
- And much more

The Skills & Expertise page is a great place to explore your industry and add skills to your profile.

Another aspect of the Skills & Expertise feature you'll want to know about is called Endorsements. Remember I was saying in Chapter 3 how important it is to get social proof to create a successful brand on LinkedIn? Well, this feature allows LinkedIn members to endorse each other's skills and expertise. Endorsing someone's skill is like giving a recommendation; however, there is no text, and it is much simpler and faster to do.

To endorse a fellow member's skills, simply scroll down on that person's profile to his Skills & Expertise section. Look at his list of skills and hover your mouse over a skill, and the text will change to *Endorse*. Click on that skill and the text will change to Endorsed! and your smiling face will then appear as an endorser right there on the profile. So not only do you help your friend gain more social proof, but you gain branding and exposure by having your photo on his profile. In addition, when someone clicks on your photo, a window will pop up with your name, professional headline, and two hyperlinks that say *View Profile* and *Invite to connect*. This will allow more users to visit your profile and see what you are all about and also invite you to become a connection.

Just as you learned in Chapter 3 about requesting recommendations, you should also add asking for endorsements to your LinkedIn strategy. Here are some guidelines to follow:

1. **Endorse others first and endorse honestly**

   You can start by endorsing the people who are in your network first, before you ask for endorsements (remember: givers get!). You'll be helping your friends see where their strengths are. But don't go overboard and endorse every skill they have listed. Put some thought into it and highlight the areas of expertise you are really willing to vouch for. Those you endorse will be notified about your kind actions, which means they might turn around and start endorsing you.

2. **Begin with your most trusted friends**

   Notify the people you know and trust the best about the Endorsement feature. Tell them that you have endorsed their skills, and ask them if they would pick a few skills of yours to endorse. Pick out the people you know well, and in this way you can slowly begin to add endorsements.

3. **No spam**

   In a situation like this, you never want to blast out an email to everyone you're connected with and ask for endorsements. Mass mailings are considered spam on LinkedIn and typically ignored. Target your requests just as you focus all your communications on LinkedIn to just the people you want to reach.

Languages

The world is shrinking, and people who speak many languages are in high demand. Make sure you add your languages by going to *Profile > Edit Profile*, than going to Languages and clicking on *+ Add a language*. (See Fig. 5-2.)

Figure 5-1. The Skills & Expertise page gives you the ability to add skills to your profile and also read a wide range of information related to your skills drawn from many sections of LinkedIn.

Education

Go to *Profile > Edit Profile > Education* and fill in the places you went to school by clicking on *+ Add a school*. You can also add activities and societies that were a part of your school days. It's important to add your school for numerous reasons. When searching for ways to build your connections, LinkedIn will display all the students who were at your school at the same time as you were and give you the opportunity to connect with them. This will enable you to get a jump-start on building your connections. If you don't fill out your school, you will miss out on this valuable way to begin adding connections.

Also, if you don't have a lot of work experience, LinkedIn gives you the ability to add recommendations to your profile right from this section. Perhaps a professor will agree to write a recommendation that will give you a chance to complete your profile. I would focus on adding colleges and vocational schools here if you can; add your high school if that is your only option.

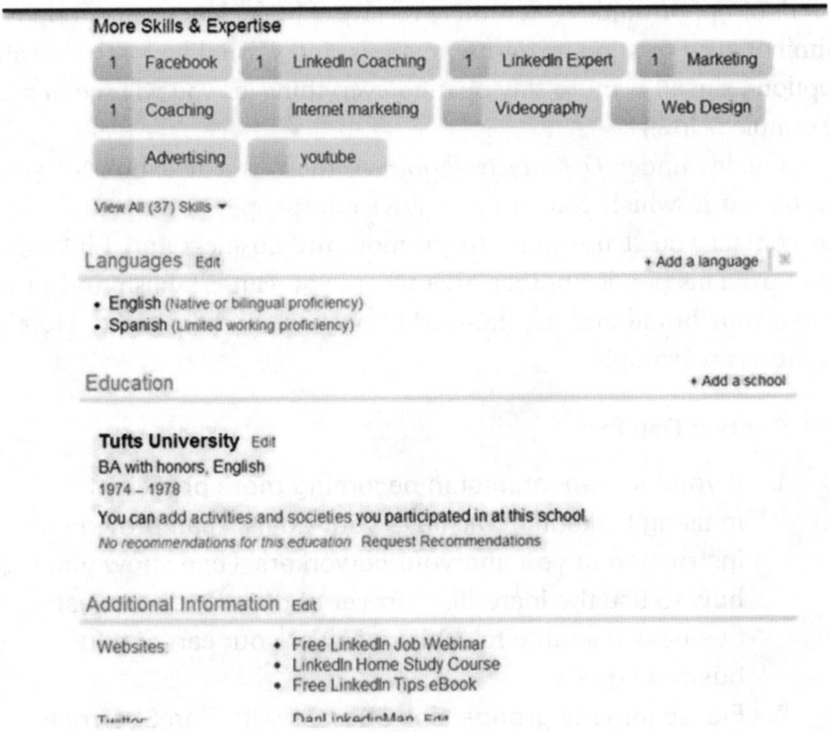

Figure 5-2. Adding and completing various sections will enable you to have a complete profile. Shown are sections for Skills & Expertise, Languages, Education, and Additional Information.

Contact

This is a key section thxat you will also find by going to *Profile > Edit Profile*. Next to where it says *Contact (Your name) for* you will see a blue hyperlink to the right that says *Change contact preferences*. Click on that to bring up a form where you can explain to your network the way in which you want to be contacted (see Figure 5-3).

First, you select what kind of messages you are open to getting. I choose the first option, saying that I'm open to all kinds of messages, since that's what LinkedIn is for...connecting with people. Second, you select your *Opportunity Preferences*, which tells your network what kinds of opportunities you want to receive. This includes career opportunities, new ventures, expertise requests, and so on. I have selected all options, since I want to stay open to everything (as you will see in my example below.)

Finally, under *Opportunity Preferences*, there is a text box for you to fill out in which you can give advice to people on how and why to contact you. I use mine to promote my business and LinkedIn groups. This box is another area where you can establish and promote your brand and tell the world how you can help them. Here's mine as an example:

Contact Dan for:

1. If you have an interest in becoming more proficient in using LinkedIn to achieve your goals, I can provide instruction to you and your coworkers. I can show you how to use the incredible power of the world's largest business resource to achieve any of your career and business goals.
2. Please join my groups Link Success with Dan Sherman and Tampa Bay Marketing Professionals.
3. Call me to set up a no-obligation, free phone consultation.
4. Make each day count. This is not a dress rehearsal.
   - career opportunities
   - consulting offers
   - new ventures
   - job inquiries
   - expertise requests
   - business deals
   - reference requests
   - getting back in touch

You can change this section as often as you want as your priorities change and you seek different opportunities. Remember to click on the blue *Save Changes* button when you are done editing this section.

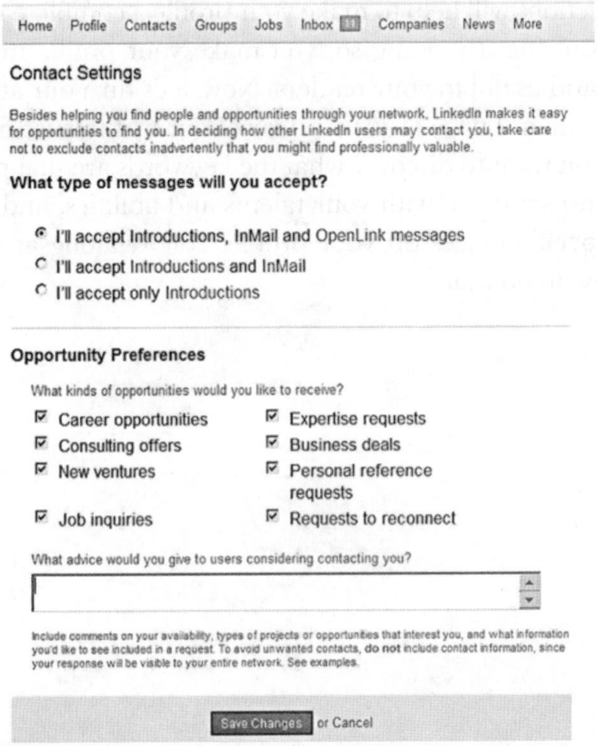

Figure 5-3. The Contact Settings box allows you to select options for the types of messages you can receive, what types of opportunities you want to be contacted for, and a text box where you can write a note to other professionals describing what opportunities you are seeking to find on LinkedIn.

Personal Information

Finally, there is also a section called Personal Information to fill out. Go to *Profile > Edit Profile*, find the section, and click on *Edit*. This is where you can put as much or as little as you want regarding your phone, address, instant message, birthday, and marital status. It's up to you what you want to put out there. I put my phone number, my city, and my birthday (no year). If you're job hunting or looking for any kind of work at all, I think it's important to put your phone number in there, but only you can decide how you want to handle your private information.

* * *

Adding sections will help to make your profile a complete marketing tool for You, Inc. By doing so, you make your profile much more complete and useful to your readers. Now, let's turn our attention to one of the main buzzwords you hear about in Internet marketing: *keywords*. You want to discover what the keywords are that people are using to find someone with your talents and abilities, and then add them to specific places on your profile. Follow along as you learn exactly how to do that.

Chapter 6: All About Keywords: Optimizing Your Profile to Be Found

Everyone has a brand. I am talking about You, Inc. What do you want to be known for? What's your specialty? What sets you apart? Once you make that decision and have it written down in a few words, then you can create your LinkedIn profile in such a way that when people are searching for someone with those skills, your profile is number one or at least on page one.

Wouldn't it be great for people to find *you* rather than you always making calls and contacting other people to achieve your goals? In this chapter, you'll learn how to make that happen, and I'll start off by using myself as an example.

I want to be known as the LinkedIn Expert. Now, I have 23 million people in my network, and when I do a simple search (by entering *LinkedIn Expert* into the search box in the upper right next to *People*), I get over 9,000 results for that term and my profile appears as number one. As a result, I get media opportunities and consulting requests just by people finding me.

Bear in mind that your search would be different. If you searched on *LinkedIn Expert* but I am not in your network, I won't show up, of course. But within my network, I do. And that means more people will click on my profile, visit my websites, download my brochure and articles, and so on. The reason I show up first is that I optimized my profile by adding in the term *LinkedIn Expert* and *LinkedIn* in several key places. Now we'll cover exactly how you can appear on page one of LinkedIn searches so you become known as the expert, gain credibility and authority status, and get the sale or job or whatever you are seeking.

Four Required Places for Your Keywords

The first step is to pick your keywords. What do you want to be found for? Next, optimize your profile by putting the keywords in the four main places that will help you show up as number one for the keywords that describe your brand or expertise. Once you make these changes in your profile, you should see some instant results in how you appear in LinkedIn searches.

When you're ready to optimize your profile, here are the four places to put your keywords to instantly move up in LinkedIn searches:

1. **Headline**
   As discussed in Chapter 2, you can make your headline a benefit statement such as:
   "I Provide the Most Comprehensive and Affordable IT Training in the State of Nevada"
   Or, if you do several things, include them with initial capital letters and use the | symbol (hit *Shift* and \ simultaneously), such as "Web Designer | Graphic Artist | Programmer | Author"
   They both work, as they both tell people how you can help them. Just be sure that you include your brand or keyword in the headline, as that is one of the key places LinkedIn considers when ranking you in searches. You will see in my profile that the first words are *LinkedIn Expert*.

2. **Current Work Experience**
   The second place LinkedIn looks is your current work experience, so make sure your current job titles have your keyword prominently displayed. I have *LinkedIn Expert* and *LinkedIn* in my current job titles, and so that helps me with rankings.

I see many people with CEO or President as job titles. If you are required through company policy to have that in your LinkedIn job title, or if you simply prefer it that way, then please leave it alone. But if you are very interested in coming up first in LinkedIn searches, you'll need to change that to a keyword, to something you do rather than what you are called.

3. **Past Work Experience**

Just as with your current jobs, you want your past jobs to have your keyword in the job title so LinkedIn moves you up in the rankings. So, maybe you're thinking that you don't have a past "job" that had that keyword. Simple: the things you list as "jobs" don't have to be full-time, nine-to-five type jobs. If you did consulting or volunteer work in that field, or anything that you could put as a "job" on LinkedIn and that has that keyword, you are all set.

On my profile, I have as past jobs some short-term LinkedIn consulting and speaking work. That enables me to use the term *LinkedIn Expert* in Past Experience and move me up in the rankings. You should try to have several past jobs with your keywords in the position titles.

4. **Summary**

Here is where you get to give your commercial for your brand, for You, Inc. Remember to make it value-driven and benefit-oriented; state how you help people and how they can reach you and hire you. You can also add a little bit about you personally in this section. For example, I have a short section that describes my philosophy on life. People want to do business with those that they know, so adding some personal thoughts is helpful.

Your summary is where you need to add keywords for your branding to make sure you show up high in the search rankings. Don't "stuff" keywords, meaning don't put in an overabundance of your keywords so that your summary is not readable as sentences. Work them in so that it still reads correctly and flows. You have 2,000 characters to use, and I suggest you use them all.

Research Your Competitors

Go ahead and make these changes today. To begin the process, I strongly suggest you do a little research first by going to the box in the upper right on any screen, selecting *People,* searching on your keyword, and seeing if you show up on page one. Then, add keywords in the places as I suggested, and check again and see if you appear on page one of LinkedIn searches.

When I did this with a local sales trainer, we searched on his keyword and he was nowhere to be found. When we added *Sales Trainer* in the four places I mentioned, his profile immediately came up number five. I also recently helped a computer expert who wanted to be found in LinkedIn searches by showing him where to put his specialty, Microsoft Access, in the four key places. He told me that before he did not appear in searches, but afterward his was the first profile when that term was searched for.

One tip: when you are doing competitive research, check out the profiles of the people who appear in the first few positions for your keyword. You'll see the keyword you searched for highlighted, and you can see just why those people showed up ahead of you. How many times do they have the keyword in their headline? In their summary? In their past and current jobs? In their specialties? You can actually count them up, and that will create a benchmark.

Follow their lead: add your keyword into your profile in the places they have on theirs and use some of their methodology. Soon if you keep tweaking your profile, you'll end up ahead of them in the search results.

Your goal is to be number one for your search term. Then you will be contacted for consulting, speaking, or other types of work when people are searching for your specialty.

Advanced Optimization Strategies

Keyword placement is really important to appear high in the search rankings, but other factors also come into play. You'll get ranked higher if you have more recommendations and more connections, so you need to be working on these as well as your keyword optimization. Having a paid profile also aids in getting ranked higher. So if you can get a premium account, I would recommend it.

Other Places to Optimize Your Profile

The four areas I mentioned are the most important places to get your keywords in to be ranked high in searches. But you can also optimize your profile by having keywords show up in the following places:

- **Recommendations.** It's helpful to have your keywords in recommendations you get, as that contributes to your profile's optimization. That's why it's a good idea to write up some bullet points with your keywords for people who agree to recommend you, or even write the whole recommendation for them and put in your keywords.
- **Websites.** You can optimize the Websites section, where you are allowed to put three websites. Put in a "call to action" to describe your site, and use your keywords. All three of my websites have the term *LinkedIn*, which is one of the main keywords I want to be found for (i.e., Free LinkedIn Tips, Learn LinkedIn Strategies, and LinkedIn Classes in Florida).
- **Public profile URL.** You can optimize your public profile URL. Go to *Profile > Edit Profile,* and at the bottom of your main information box, you will see a small LinkedIn "in" logo by your profile URL and the hyperlink *Edit.* Click on that, go to the Public Profile page, and find the box on the right called *Your public profile URL.* You can add your keyword to the end of your URL, as I have done (mine is *linkedin/in/ linkedinspeaker*).
- **Groups.** Join groups with your keyword in the title, since your list of groups shows up in your profile. You can join up to 50 groups, so you can have many with your keyword.

- **Skills.** Add your keywords in the Skills & Expertise section. Add them automatically by going to *More > Skills & Expertise* on the top menu bar and entering them on the Skills & Expertise page.
- **Interests.** Here's another great spot to optimize your profile, although I see very few people using this as a strategy. I use it to get found in searches on LinkedIn, and it's very effective. In the Interests area in the Additional Information section, you have a text area where you can write quite a bit about what your interests are. You should definitely put your keywords in this spot, but here's an additional idea.

   In my profile, I list LinkedIn because it's a huge interest and using the term helps me with optimization. But in this area I also put the names of all the social media and LinkedIn experts I follow who have high brand-name recognition. I'm interested in them, so doing so makes sense. But by having their names on my profile, I also get found when people are searching for them.

   Perhaps someone is looking for a social media speaker and when they search for another expert by name, I come up. If I'm available to speak and the other expert is not, I can put myself in contention for the opportunity. If you're interested in this strategy, search on your keywords in the People search, find the names of all the experts who appear on the first page, and then add their names as your interests.

Where *Not* to Optimize Your Profile

As you look around on LinkedIn, you will run into profiles where the person has endeavored to optimize his or her name field. For example, adding words by their name such as:

Billy Bob Thornton | Tattoo Lover | Wild Man | Movie Star | Musician

I recommend you do not put anything extra in the name field such as keywords, phone numbers, or email addresses, as it is against the

LinkedIn Terms and Conditions (T&Cs) and you really want to stay on their good side. I'll give you a story to demonstrate.

Once, I had to contact customer service with a question. At the time I had optimized my name field with:

Dan Sherman | Speaker and Trainer

I got a note back from customer service, not with an answer to a request, but with a strict warning that I was in violation of their T&Cs with my name field. So I had to change it and then write back with my question, which they then answered, but it was a delay for me. Now, many people optimize their name field or even add their phone number, e-mail address, or LION (see Chapter 7), but for me, my name is branding enough.

I'm confident in my name as my brand, I don't need to embellish it, and I want to stay on the right side of the LinkedIn rules. I'm sharing my experience with you so you can make your own judgment call on this.

Moving Sections in Your Profile

Working on your profile is an ongoing process. You are never quite done, since there are always ways to improve the content and optimization. One strategy you can experiment with is moving entire sections around until they are in the order that best suits your needs.

We touched on this briefly before. But I want to go over it again because it's really important to modify your profile so it fits your career goals, and not just leave sections in their default positions.

Once you have built a very robust profile with lots of sections and applications, decide what it is that is most important for people to see when they land on your profile. You can drag and drop entire sections like Summary, Applications, or Experience simply by hovering your mouse over the heading of the section, waiting until the four arrow "crosshairs" gunsight-like symbol appears, and dragging and dropping to your heart's content (be sure to be in *Profile > Edit Profile* mode).

Personally, I put applications first in my profile, since I like having my testimonial videos and downloadable articles front and center. One word on the Applications section: the box that contains your applications moves as one unit. You can't move, say, SlideShare to the top of your profile and put Box.net on the bottom. The entire application block goes together. I find this a very small inconvenience.

I've seen people put their Personal Information section first because they want their contact information prominent; others put their Experience first to showcase their career accomplishments; still others lead with their Summary. It just depends on your LinkedIn goals. What do you want your prospective client, partner, investor, customer, or manager to see first? You should arrange your sections in the order that will best position you to your target audience.

* * *

Now that you have added sections and applications and completely filled out your profile, you've created your own little piece of real estate on LinkedIn of which you can be proud. It truly displays all that you are capable of offering to the world, and you want everyone who might potentially do business with you to stop by and partake of all the information. Only people who are in your network can see your profile, so how do your grow your network to maximum its effectiveness? Coming up I'll explain how to create a first-class network that will be the cornerstone of your LinkedIn strategy.

Chapter 7: Your Virtual Rolodex: Grow Your Network by Adding Contacts

As a professional speaker, I am always looking for ways to improve my skills, and for a long time I was a member of the largest speaking organization, National Speakers Association. One year our national conference was held in Orlando and one of our presenters was Harvey Mackay, the famous author and successful company president. He was promoting his new book on networking, *Dig Your Well Before You're Thirsty*. A master networker, Harvey Mackey urged all of us to make sure that no matter the state of our current work situation, we should always be adding contacts to our database so that we have the people we need when we're ready to reach out for partners, employers, advisors, investors, and anyone else who could assist us.

To me that is the beauty of LinkedIn. By getting involved on the site, you are actively building a huge database of professionals around the globe who can provide assistance to you when the need arises. Whether you are just starting out on LinkedIn or have been active for a while, you can see how well you've dug *your* well by going to the top toolbar and clicking *Home > LinkedIn Home*. About halfway down in the right-hand column, you will see: YOUR LINKEDIN NETWORK. You will see the number for your total first-level connections, another number revealing how many total people are in your network (first-, second-, and third-level connections combined), and how many new people have joined your network recently. (Refer back to Chapter 1 for the discussion on understanding the LinkedIn levels.)

500 Is the Magic Number

Check your first-level connection number and see what is there. If it is not a robust number, not to worry. There are plenty of ways to grow your connections. Your first objective is get out of the single digits and get to at least 500. This is because the number of your LinkedIn connections is prominently displayed in the top information box on your profile that people scan first when they come to learn about you. If you have less than 500 connections—say 100—people will assume that you are not a well-connected person. This may label you as someone who does not have much value when they are deciding whether to add you to their LinkedIn network or even to hire you or work with you.

Until you get to 500, you are not going to be perceived as a real active LinkedIn user, and consequently not as a strong potential connection or a "player" in the LinkedIn world. But once you get to 500, LinkedIn stops counting on your profile and puts "500+". That means you could have 501 or 5001; it will still say "500+". You want every aspect of your profile to reflect well on you. Try to get to 500 as soon as you can so you're "in the club."

Adding connections brings other benefits. When you connect with more people, it extends your second- and third-level connections until you are literally connected with millions of professionals around the globe. (About 50 percent of LinkedIn users are in the United States; the others are spread out worldwide.) That means there are millions of people who can find you, hire you, offer you publicity opportunities, partner with you, invest in your firm, and help you with any business goal you have. Without a large network, you won't have many people who can reach you, read your profile, learn about you, or work with you.

Having a large network makes you a desirable connection and someone whom people will want to add to their network. That's because when they connect with you, they increase their network of connections. Your first-level connections become their second-level connections, and your second-level connections become their thirds.

To Connect or Not to Connect

The debate of whether to connect with people you don't know or connect only with people you know sometimes takes on the seriousness of Hamlet's soliloquy in Shakespeare's tragedy that begins: "To be or not to be." You'll find proponents on both sides. But in my mind, there's no argument. I'm firmly in the camp of the "open networkers," and I believe you should connect with everyone you can. Doing so simply expands your network and your opportunities. You can look at more profiles and contact more people, and more people can contact you. Massive connecting speeds up and enhances all your networking goals.

If you connect only with those people you know, people in your city, or those you grew up with, you'll be stuck in that same circle and won't be exposed to new opportunities. A great example of opening up your opportunities happened to me recently when I connected with a networking guru in England. He was able to read my profile and see that I'm well versed in LinkedIn, and he invited me to an interview on his podcast on the subject of networking.

I did the interview, and now people in England are aware of me and my products and services and are buying my online courses. Had I turned down his connection invitation because I did not know him, I would not have had the opportunity, and this is just one of many examples from my experience. I get consulting requests from Japan, Czechoslovakia, and India as well as from around the good ol' USA because I am an open networker and I work to broaden my network with people from around the world whom I don't know.

How to Get More Connections

Let's get to the heart of this: whom do you invite, and how? First, you should know that LinkedIn allots all new users 3,000 invitations to use for connecting with people, and limits users to 30,000 users in terms of how many first-level connections we can have. The 3,000 is flexible because when someone runs out of invitations, he or she can write to Customer Service by clicking on the *Help Center* hyperlink on the menu at the bottom of any page and request more. The 30,000 number is fixed; I have not seen LinkedIn waive that yet (and, yes, I do have a contact with 30,000 connections).

In my experience, I have been allotted more invitations four times. I am very careful to stay on LinkedIn's good side, meaning I follow the rules and I write them a nice note requesting more invites. The number of reallocations has varied; before I got a premium account, I would be given an additional few hundred new invites each time. After I got a premium account, on my fourth request, I got 3,000 more invitations to use.

Avoid the Dreaded *Report Spam*

I also make sure I have no black marks on my record by inviting only people that I'm fairly sure will connect with me. I work hard not to get any *Report Spam*'s. That's when you invite someone and she clicks *Report Spam*. When you get a few of these, you get into LinkedIn's doghouse; the site places restrictions on your account, and it hurts you when you ask for more invites.

How do I avoid *Report Spam*'s? I either invite people I know or specifically invite other open networkers to connect. Open networkers have a code: they never click *Report Spam* when they get an invitation, no matter who it is from. I'll be talking later about how to find open networkers, as they will be crucial to you in terms of building up a large network.

What if you invite someone and he or she never responds? Can you take the invitation back and invite someone else? The answer is yes. Click on *Contacts* on the top menu bar, and LinkedIn will display all your first-level connections. On the very bottom, you will see a hyperlink that says *Sent invitations*. Click on it and you will see everyone you ever invited and whether each person accepted or not. If you see someone who did not accept, you can click on the invite to review it, then click a button that says *Withdraw.* The person is not notified, and you get the invite back. If people do not respond, it might mean that they don't want to connect, or it could be that they don't check their LinkedIn inbox much. You can always send them a regular email to let them know you are trying to connect.

How to Start Inviting Contacts

The place to begin is on the top toolbar. Click on *Contacts > Add Connections.* You will notice *See Who You Already Know on LinkedIn* and a place to put an email address, such as a Gmail, Hotmail, Yahoo-Mail, or AOL address (see Figure 7-1). When you put in your own email address and password and click *Continue,* LinkedIn searches your email database and finds all your contacts. It identifies which people are already on LinkedIn by matching their email address with their LinkedIn accounts. You will see a small blue box next to those already on LinkedIn. Go ahead and invite your email contacts who are already on the site. Do not have any concerns about spamming or losing control, because LinkedIn will never automatically invite people in your address book; you need to do it.

You can also import an email list from programs such as Outlook or Apple Mail. Click on *Any Email* below the envelope icon. When you do,

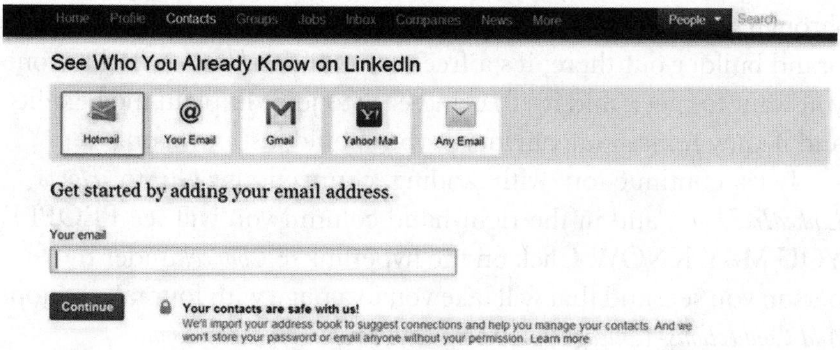

Figure 7-1. On the Add Connections tab is the area to enter your email address and see whom you know who is already on LinkedIn. Also in this tab you are able to import desktop emails and invite someone by using his or her email address.

you will see a section called *More ways to connect*. There you will see two hyperlinks. Click on *Upload contacts file* and you can browse your hard drive and upload a file. Click on *Invite by individual email* and a box will open where you can type in email addresses or cut and paste a list.

When looking through the list of your current contacts, I recommend that you do not invite anyone to join you who is not on LinkedIn already. It's really a waste of an invitation because that person is not going to know what LinkedIn is, and he or she will ignore you, thinking the site is some meaningless thing. (If they only knew!) It involves some time on your part to explain to people who are not on LinkedIn why they should join, so do this on an as-needed basis (for example, when you want a recommendation).

Personally, I have had mixed results convincing my email contacts who don't use LinkedIn to use it. Some people have indicated to me that they are very cautious with their privacy and refuse to join any social network at all. Others say that they have a job and don't need a job-hunting site (cue Mr. Mackay). Because there are so many people using LinkedIn with whom to connect, I don't spend any time trying to convince people to join so I can connect with them.

If you do feel like making the effort, as in the case where you want a recommendation from them, you can enlighten them to the fact that LinkedIn lets you stay in contact with people even if they change jobs; it helps you find an amazing array of opportunities through your extended network; it is the most powerful personal brand builder out there; it's a free research database to find anyone you want to meet; and it's free and easy to join. Explain the benefits, and if they remain unconvinced, you should just move on.

Let's continue on with adding connections. Go to *Home > LinkedIn Home*, and in the right-hand column you will see PEOPLE YOU MAY KNOW. Click on the hyperlink + *Connect* under the first person you see, and that will take you to a page with four tabs on top: *Add Connections, Colleagues, Alumni,* and *People You May Know.*

The *Add Connections* tab takes you to the page we have already discussed in How to Start Inviting Connections. This is where you enter your email address and LinkedIn lets you know which of your current contacts are already on the site.

Click on *Colleagues*, and everyone who worked at each company you listed in Experience (your job history) during the time you were there will appear. This gives you a very easy way to build your connections, since you know them and they are on LinkedIn right now.

Tab over to *Alumni* and that brings up a screen displaying all your school classmates who attended the school when you were there. That's why it's important to add where you went to school in the Education section. Again, these will be people you know who are already on LinkedIn, and they are good to invite.

The final tab to the right is *People You May Know*. Take a look through and see if LinkedIn has identified people you know who are on the site already. If you know them, invite them. If you don't recognize any names, I would ignore this. You do not want to risk getting a *Report Spam* and blemishing your LinkedIn record.

Click back to the page showing the four tabs and you'll discover a way to monitor your sent invitations. On the very far right is a hyperlink that says *View Sent Invitations*. Here is where you manage your sent invitations and can withdraw some if you wish.

Remember, the larger your network, the more powerful LinkedIn becomes in terms of helping you achieve whatever business goal you have. If you have only 100 people in your network because you are happy about knowing each person and their families in depth, remember that these 100 people have probably referred all the business opportunities, prospects, and friends that you are going to get from them. So it pays to widen your connections as far and wide as you can.

Creative Ways to Get More Connections

Once you've gone through your email lists, schools, and past jobs, you should have a base on which to build your first-level connection database. The more connections you have, the more people get added to your network on a daily basis through second- and third-level connections.

Building your connections should become part of your daily routine. Here are some strategies for how to get more first-level connections on LinkedIn.

Networking

When you come home from a networking event with a stack of business cards, don't just chuck them into a shoebox. These are people you can add to your database on LinkedIn. The morning after the event, take your cards, look up each person on LinkedIn, and see who is not yet a first-level connection. Now you can send each person a personalized invitation, and if LinkedIn prompts you to add the person's email address, you've got it right there on the card. By doing it the very next morning, you will be top of that person's mind, and he or she won't have forgotten you.

In terms of the personalized invitation, understand that LinkedIn will give you a standard message you can send that says, "I'd like to add you to my network." Whenever possible, you should strive to personalize your connection messages. It will make the people receiving them feel much more appreciated. Each one will know that he or she is not just another number in your database but a living, breathing human being different from any other on the planet. So go ahead and remind those people how you met, what impressed you about them, and how you might work together. For example:

> Hi Joe. It was great to meet you last night at the big charity event. Great entertainment, huh? How about those fire eaters and jugglers? I enjoyed our conversation about the correlation between start-up creation and Moore's law. Let's have coffee soon and see how we might be able to share leads. And please connect with me here on LinkedIn. Thank you.

On the Web

If you have a personal blog or website, you have a great place to put a hyperlink to your LinkedIn profile. Use your public profile

URL, which you can copy by going to *Profile* > *View Profile* and copying the link in the bottom of your main information box.

When people click on the link, they are connected to your profile and can read all about you and how you help people, and since every profile has a button that says *Connect,* you can get more people connecting with you. So make sure you have links to your profile on all your online sites, including other social media sites like Facebook and Twitter, with a call to action near the URL stating, "Connect with me on LinkedIn."

Do you send a lot of email? Put your public profile URL in the email signature so that everyone you write to can connect with you.

Do you have an email newsletter? Many of us do, and it's the perfect place to ask for connections. I use iContact, but you may use Aweber, Constant Contact, MailChimp, or another program. Put a link to your LinkedIn profile where you can write an inviting message such as:

> I would love for you to connect with me on LinkedIn. I am building my network, and would be very happy to introduce you to anyone in my network who could be of assistance to you.

On Your Business Cards

Make it easy for people to find and connect with you on LinkedIn. Include your public profile URL on your card so that people you meet at networking events will be able to easily invite you to connect.

During Your LinkedIn Networking

Another way to meet people to connect with you on LinkedIn is something that will happen naturally. As you network with other professionals in LinkedIn groups or ask or answer questions in Linked-In Answers, you are constantly meeting like-minded people. It is a natural occurrence that you will strike up online conversations with these people and agree to become first-level connections. The more active you are on LinkedIn, the more this will happen, which adds to the size of your personal database.

For example, when you meet someone on LinkedIn in Groups or Answers that you want to invite, you will click on that person's name and be taken to his or her profile. From there, simply click on the button marked *Connect.* Then write something on the page in which you request a connection reminding that person about your interaction on LinkedIn and why you want to connect.

Open Networkers: The Key to Hypergrowth

Now we come to the secret weapon for creating a huge network on LinkedIn, and that is by joining open networking groups. The first one you should join is TopLinked, the largest. On the top toolbar, go to *Groups > Group Directory.* Type in *TopLinked* in the keyword search bar and it will be the first group that appears (see Figure 7-2). (You can also type TopLinked into the search box on the upper right by first selecting groups.)

Go ahead and join the group. Once you do, look in the *Manager's choice* box on the far right for a discussion titled *The most recently updated TopLinked invite me list.* This list is the ticket to rapidly growing your first-level connections. This is a list of many of the open networkers on LinkedIn. When you click on it, you now have two options, a free account or a paid account.

For my first three years on LinkedIn, I had the TopLinked free account. By signing up for one, you get Excel spreadsheets every week with about 2,000 total emails of open networkers—people who have agreed to be on the list with the clear understanding that they will *not* click *Report Spam* when you invite them, so they are safe to invite even though you don't know them.

I suggest you sign up for the free account first. When you get the lists, which will show up in the email account you used to register with TopLinked (not your LinkedIn inbox), save them on your computer in a place you can easily find them, such as on your desktop. (All you need to invite someone to connect with you on LinkedIn is his or her email address.)

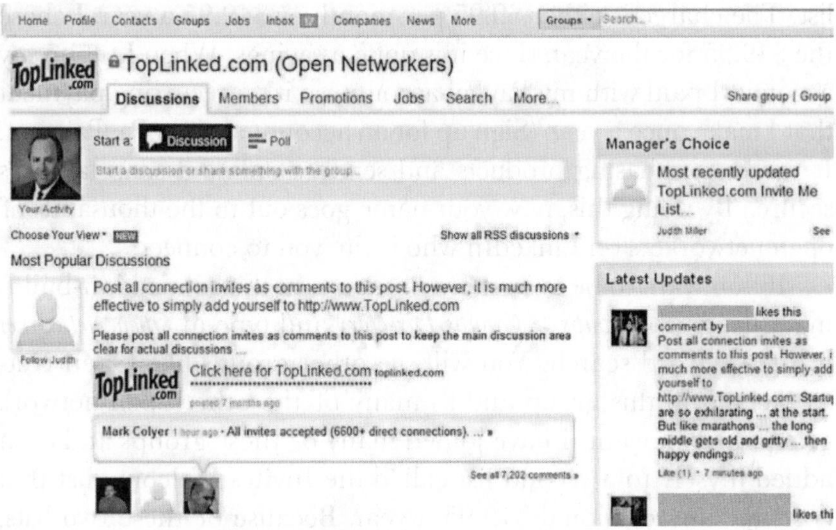

Figure 7-2. By joining the TopLinked group, you can connect with other open networkers and dramatically increase the size of your LinkedIn network.

Then, open up LinkedIn and click on *Contacts > Add Connections*. You will see *Any Email* under an envelope icon, so click on that. Toward the bottom of the next page, you will find a hyperlink saying *Invite by individual email,* and when you click on that, you will see an open text box with *Type email addresses below, separated by commas.* Now it's up to you as to how proactive you will be about adding contacts, but as a general rule I would say it's best to invite only 50 people a day. What I do is copy 50 emails at a time onto my Notepad on my PC, (if you are on a PC, click on the *Start* button on the lower left of the desktop and click on *Notepad*), add commas after each name, then copy and paste the list into the open text box and click *Send Invitations.* By using this method, you will grow your network fast.

Getting a Paid Open Networking Account

If you want to grow your first-level connections even faster, you can get a paid TopLinked account and add your name to the "invite me" list. The charge is either $9.95 per month or $49.95 a year. I chose the $49.95 for the year, since it is quite a savings. When I set up my account, I paid with my PayPal account, so it's a recurring payment that I make once a year. (Sign up for an account at www.PayPal.com. It makes purchasing products and services online a snap, and it's secure.) By doing this, now your name goes out to the thousands of open networkers on LinkedIn who invite you to connect.

If you want to be even more proactive in the connection-building area, go to *Groups > Groups Directory* and type in *Open Networker* in the keyword search. You will see other groups like Open Networkers. Join this group and as many of the other open network groups as you want. I have joined many of these groups and even added myself to a second list called the Invites Welcome list that costs me an additional $19.95 a year. Because of these two lists, I get about 30 invitations a day, which helps me grow my network fast.

As you spend time on LinkedIn, you will see that people advertise the fact that they are open networkers with the acronym "LION" (LinkedIn Open Networker). They'll sometimes even put it in their name field, such as "Betty Smith | LION." Or they will put it in their professional headline under their name.

I don't put LION in my name field or my headline. First, it is against the terms of LinkedIn to add anything but your name to your name field. Second, there are lots and lots of LIONS on LinkedIn, and I don't feel it's special enough to warrant taking up space in my headline. That's why I let people know I'm an open networker within my profile summary.

By taking advantage of TopLinked and the other open networking groups, you can rapidly expand your network. If you have only a few connections, your total reach will be small. Once you get up to thousands of connections, when you check your statistics (*Home > LinkedIn Home*), you'll see that your network has millions and millions of people. That means millions of people who can find you, read your profile, and present opportunities to you. Go forth and grow your network!

*   *   *

One of the benefits of growing your first-level connections into the thousands is that inevitably you will end up with millions of professionals in your network of contacts. That means you'll have lots of people you can connect with and look for opportunities. Let's get into finding the people you want to meet and getting in touch with them, which is discussed in the next chapter.

Chapter 8: Your Social Influence Circle: Searching For and Contacting People

We've spent a good bit of time dealing with how to optimize your profile with keywords so you can be found for opportunities. Now that you have created a profile that will show up high in LinkedIn searches, and you've made sure it's value-oriented so that when people visit it, they will want to learn more about you, let's cover the proactive side of LinkedIn: finding and contacting people.

First, expand your thinking about whom you can find on Linked-In. Don't think of it as only a place to find customers, although that may be your primary focus. You can also find partners to work on projects, and they may be interested in sharing leads. For example, a great person to connect with is what's called a "Center of Influence," someone with connections and a client base similar to the prospects you want to reach.

Here's how it works: if you're a financial advisor, you might connect with a lawyer or a banker in your location and see if you can create a mutual lead-sharing system. Whatever your occupation, look for non-competing professionals who share the same kinds of clients as you do. Contact them and set up a meeting where you can propose creating a potential lead-sharing group. Then perhaps once a month you can get together and share leads. You don't need to be in business alone. With LinkedIn, you can share OPC—other people's connections (or clients).

There are so many different types of helpful connections you can make on LinkedIn. For example:

- Look for service providers for your business. I have hired consultants to help me on a project basis after being impressed with posts they made in Groups.
- Find people who can help you with a project, either as a part-time or a full-time employee.
- Locate an expert who can advise you on a critical part of your business.
- Connect with people in your industry, and set up a phone call to talk shop and see if there is any basis for a joint venture.
- Find speaking gigs or a speaker for your event.
- Search for employees, investors, vendors, partners, suppliers, donors for your cause, board members, and strategic influencers.
- Create an advisory board with top thought leaders.

Remember that everyone is on LinkedIn to network and do business, so don't be afraid to reach out when you have a need. Contact those people whose posts in Groups and Answers impressed you the most. Click on their profile, find their contact information, and give them a call or send an email.

Using Advanced People Search

In addition to finding people to meet in Groups or in the Answers section, you can also use the very powerful Advanced People Search. In the search box in the top right, select *People* and then click on the word *Advanced* to the right of the magnifying glass to bring up the Advanced Search Form (see Figure 8-1).

Begin your search with keywords. What keyword will your intended "target" have in his or her profile? If it contains several words, put the keyword in "quotation marks" so that LinkedIn does not return profiles with the words in different areas of the profile.

Let's say you sell to human resources managers. You would type "*Human Resources*" into the keyword box, but that would bring up thousands of people. So you use the whole Advanced Search Form to narrow your focus, by filling in the location, the industry, and the relationship to you (choose first, second, or third level or your whole network).

Having a premium account will give you more options to narrow your search. You can get granular by selecting the person's title, company size, where in the Fortune 1000 that person's company is ranked (according to size of company), and what kinds of contacts he or she wants to receive; you can even search individually through your groups.

If you have a premium account, you can give LinkedIn additional search commands; that is, you can also select how you want the keyword search to be conducted. In your premium account, scroll all the way down to the bottom of the Advanced Search Form page and you will see a *Sort* drop-down menu. You can sort by:

- **Relevance.** This sort method returns the people whose profiles have the keyword you selected. The sort will display profiles first that have many instances of the keyword, premium members, and your first-, second-, and third-level connections.
- **Relationship.** This shows how closely they are connected to you by level—first level, then second level, and so on—so you will get the people who are easiest to contact displayed first.
- **Relationship and Recommendations.** This sorts by how closely the people are connected and by how many recommendations they have received.
- **Connections.** This sorts profiles in order of how many first-level connections they have, so you get the most connected people displayed on top.
- **Keywords.** This sorts profiles with the best match to your keyword, whether they are connected to your network or not. This is helpful only when you do not care if the people are in your network or not. However, if they are not in your network, it is harder to reach them.

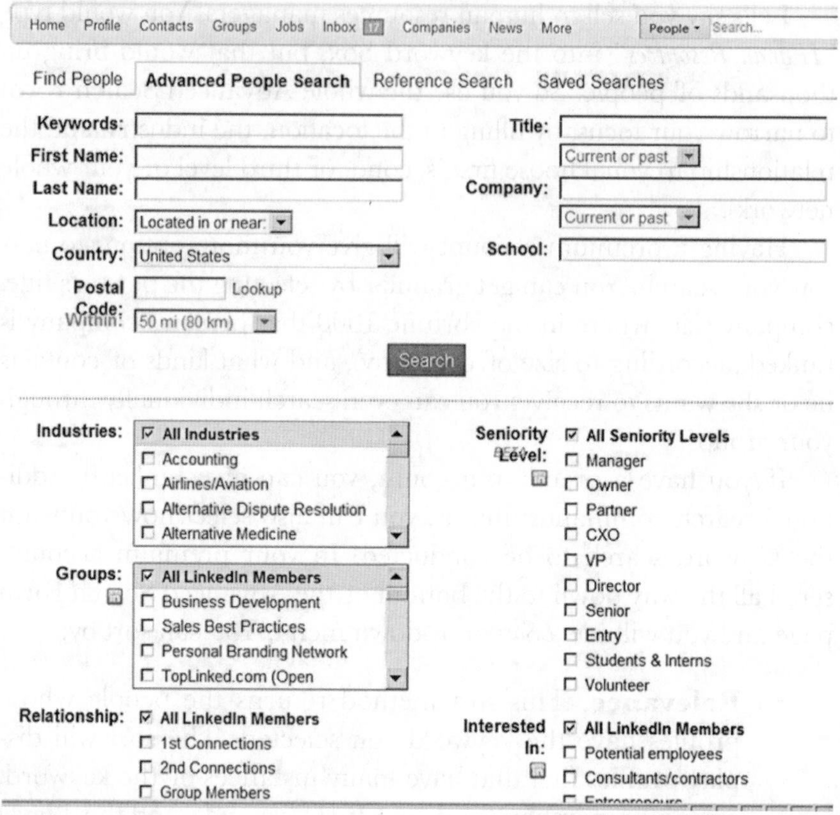

Figure 8-1. The Advanced People Search is your ticket to exploring the LinkedIn database and finding exactly the right people to connect with in order to pursue opportunities. With a premium account, you get many more options to sort the search results (premium sections are indicated by the gold "in" box).

Using the whole form, I would do a search for the keyword *"Human Resources"*, with seniority selected as *Manager* in companies with 51 to 200 people, within 50 miles of me, and it brings up 100 results. That's a lot better than when I just typed in the keyword *"Human Resources"* and got 690,000 results!

You want to use various criteria to narrow down your list. If you want to make the most of the search function, then by all means get a premium account because it offers so many more ways to narrow your focus to just the people you want to contact and those who are the easiest for you to reach.

That's targeting just keywords or occupations. Let's say I wanted to target a certain company. If I wanted to sell my product to a human resources executive at Disney, for example, I would go to the Advanced Search Form and type in my keyword *"Human Resources"*, type in *Disney* in the company box, select *Current* from the drop-down menu (because in this search I want to reach only people who currently have that job), and hit *Search*. My results come up as 783 human resources people in Disney, so I would want to refine that a little bit by location. I add in the zip code for Disney in Orlando, which is 32380. That brings the number down to about 300 people, which is more manageable.

Of course, my search results are going to be different from yours, since we all have different networks. But the overriding fact is clear: the more people you have as first-level connections, the larger your total network will be and the more people you can search for. That's why I recommend being an open networker. If you have just a few people in your first level, you will not be getting the same number of profiles to look at in the results that I get.

Save Your Search

If the search you did creates a helpful database of prospects, potential partners, or whomever you are looking for, LinkedIn lets you save the search. Click on the + *Save Search* on the far right next to the number of results (see Figure 8.2). LinkedIn then gives you the option of getting an email notification weekly or monthly when someone new who meets those search criteria pops up in your network, and those covers first-, second-, and third-level contacts as well as groups. With a free account, you can save up to three searches, and premium accounts let you save even more. Because your network grows every day, you should run your saved search daily by clicking on *Saved Searches* (the fourth tab over on the Advanced Search Form) to see what new names pop up.

What you've done is create a perpetual prospecting machine for yourself. When LinkedIn notifies you of new people who meet your exact criteria, you can read their profiles and get in touch with them and let the magic of networking begin! Know what keywords you want, experiment until you find the right ones, and build your database of prospects as big as you can.

Figure 8-2. After you've done a people search, you can click on + *Save Search* in the upper right to save the search criteria and return and run the search over and over again to capture new names.

Making a Personal Connection

Once you have identified whom you want to meet, whether it's someone you find in a Group, LinkedIn Answers, or the Advanced People Search just described, you want to—as the old phone commercial used to say—"reach out and touch someone." Take a look at that person's profile for clues on how and with what method he wants to be contacted. First, take a look at the Contact section in his profile to see what he put as his contact preferences. It will say, *Contact (name) for business deals, consulting opportunities* (or something similar). This will be a guide for you as to how to approach this person.

Sometimes a person will put her phone number and email address in that section, or perhaps that information will be in her summary. If you have a number or email address, use it tactfully to reach your target. If the person is a first-level connection, you have the opportunity to message her directly. In the information box at the top of her profile, look for the blue button that says *Send a message*. Click on it, and a dialogue box will appear where you can craft your message and send it off by pressing the blue *Send Message* button.

When sending people messages on LinkedIn, be sure that you first read their profiles. Then craft a personalized message explaining what you discovered in their profiles that leads you to believe they would benefit from an association with you. Thank them for their time in reading your message. Be brief and to the point so you're respectful of their time. Always remember to add what's in it for them if they decide to get back to you or accept an invitation to connect with you.

For example, you might write:

> We are first-level connections, and I read your profile and was impressed with what you are doing in the areas of (fill in the blank). I want to explore how we can work together, because I feel I have a solution that might greatly enhance your ability to achieve your goals (add here what they will gain, e.g., save money, save time, increase profits). Would you be open to connecting here on LinkedIn? Also, can we set up a brief telephone call?

The worst thing you can do is make this assumption: *Oh, this person will never want to talk to me.* Why would you think that? Whenever I make an assumption that someone does not want to have a conversation with me, I think back to the old chestnut from sales training: "The word *assume* stands for *Making an ass out of u (you) and me.*"

Here's an example. I was giving a LinkedIn training, and a student in the class was a commercial mortgage broker who was new to the site. He challenged me by saying, "Dan, I've got all these first-level connections. What the heck do I do with them?"

"Why don't you write to them?" I countered.

"Oh, they will never respond," he said.

"Try it," I told him.

"What do I say?" he asked. I told him to tell the people what it was in their profiles that made him want to write and ask them to please have a conversation with them.

Right then he sent a direct message to a commercial Realtor in another state where he wanted to do business. He told him he felt there were some great opportunities in his city and asked if he would be open to a phone call. Within seconds, the Realtor responded with his phone number and asked my student to call him immediately. The look on my student's face was priceless.

Can I promise this type of results every time? Of course not. But that's what LinkedIn is for: connecting with people. You won't know until you try.

Contacting Non-First-Level Connections

If you and someone else are not first-level connections and there is no contact information available in the other person's profile, the next step is to look at his information box and see if he is an Open-Link member. (All premium account holders have the option to be in OpenLink.) You will see a small circle of colored dots to the right of that person's name. That means you can send him a message directly without being a first-level connection.

If he is not in OpenLink, look at the bottom of the information box, where you will see a gray button that says *Send (name) an InMail.* InMail is the internal LinkedIn email system whereby you can contact anyone on LinkedIn who is in your network and is a second- or third-level connection. That's the good news. The "bad" news is, InMails cost money! LinkedIn is a public company and has to please its shareholders!

If you have the basic free account, you can buy InMails for $10 each. The benefit of an InMail over a cold call is that it includes a link to your profile so the recipient can read your profile and respond to you knowing who you are. If the person doesn't respond in seven days, you get the InMail credit back and you can InMail some-one else. A premium account includes InMails: Business account ($24.95/month) gives you three a month; Business Plus ($49.95/month) gives you 10 a month; and the super deluxe plan, Executive ($99.95/month), gives you 25 a month. Recruiters love the plans with lots of InMails so they can reach out to lots of potential hires, but anyone can take advantage of those premium plans. InMails roll over to the next month if they are unused.

What's great about InMails is they are instantaneous. They go right into the person's LinkedIn inbox. If you have not passed out on the floor after seeing the prices, then go ahead and purchase a premium account and include InMails in your LinkedIn prospecting and networking strategy. But if you are shocked and dismayed, don't worry. There are other avenues for reaching non-first-level connec-tions, including getting an introduction from a first-level contact.

Reaching a Second-Level Connection

The introduction feature shows you who in your first-level connec-tions is connected to your "target" person. Let's say your target is a second-level connection. In the information box in his profile, you will see a gray button that says *Send (name) an InMail* and on the right of this button a drop-down arrow. Click on it, and you will see a link that says *Get introduced* (see Figure 8-3). When you select that link, the Introduction Request Form will appear, giving you a list of first-level connections who can introduce you to your "target." Scan the list for someone you know personally. He will be the person you will ask to send your introduction to your intended contact (see Figure 8-4). Click on his name and he moves to the top of the form between you and the person you want to meet.

Fill in the subject of your request, then tell your first-level contact why you want to be introduced. I recommend reading the profile of your target connection, discovering what his goals might be, and explaining why connecting with you will help your target contact achieve his goals.

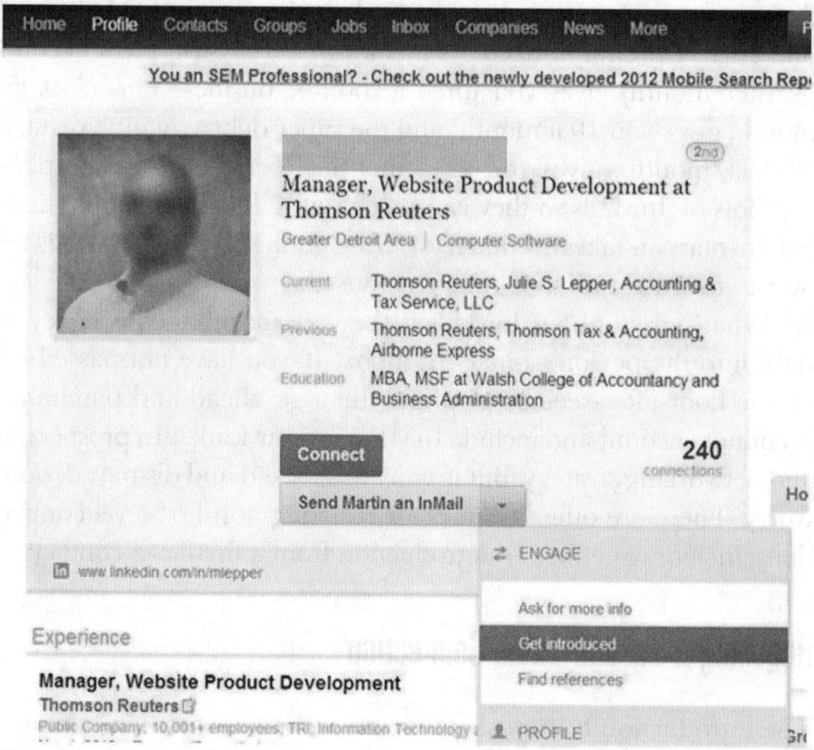

Figure 8-3. When you see a second-level connection you want to meet, you can send him an InMail or you can see how you are connected to him. Click the down arrow on the gray button in their information box and select *Get introduced* to see the names of first-level connections who can potentially introduce you.

Before you send off your message, you can check how many introductions you have left. The number you have depends on what kind of account you have. Basic free account holders get 5 outstanding introductions a month; Business members get 15; Business Plus members get 25; and the top of the heap Executive members get a whopping 35. You can always check the number of your remaining InMails and introductions by clicking on the drop-down menu under your name in the upper right of any page, and clicking on *Settings.* When someone you have asked to be introduced to accepts and you make a connection, that introduction is then freed up for you to make another introduction request.

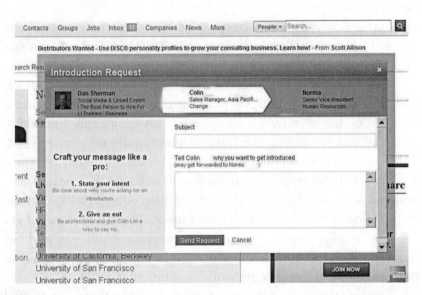

Figure 8-4. On the Introduction Request form, you can select the first-level connection you want to help you reach a second-level connection and explain the reason for your request.

Reaching a Third-Level Connection

What if the person you want to reach is a third-level connection, a friend of a friend of a friend? It works the same way, but your chances of a solid connection go down a little bit since your introduction request must pass through two people. But it is still possible.

Everyone on LinkedIn is there to network, and it really is very little work to pass on an introduction. I always pass on any introduction request I get, since I know the final recipient has the option to expand her network and meet someone new or pass depending on her current needs.

So if you land on a third-level connection's profile and it's someone you want to meet, don't despair. Click on the down arrow on the gray button in her information box that's next to *Send (name) an InMail*. Then click on the *Get introduced* link to reveal the Introduction Request Form. LinkedIn will display a list of your first-level connections who can start the introduction process. Click on the person you want to start the process. You will then see the place to put the subject of your request and a note to your first-level contact explaining why you want to be introduced. The introduction request will go to your first-level connection, who will pass it on to a connection who will pass it on to your intended target connection.

In the process of reaching out to a second- or third-level contact, your first-level connection will get your request and then can add a message of her own before she passes it on—hopefully something nice that will encourage the final recipient to act on your request. The request will show up in your first-level contact's inbox, and since you get only five introduction requests a month with the free account, you may wish to follow up with your first-level connection so that the request does not languish in his or her inbox. I send any request I get on to the next person immediately, but everyone is different and has different demands on his or her time so be sure to follow up if you can. Remember, everyone networks at different speeds.

The nice thing about the introduction feature is that it's respectful of the time of your first-level contacts. You are not calling them and interrupting them with your request; they can review it and deal with it when they are doing their LinkedIn mail. They can write a nice introduction for you, and if they do, the person you want to reach is more likely to connect with you. A request to a third level is more complicated, but it is still heads above a cold call. I have found that even though LinkedIn is a gigantic network with over 175 million people, there is an unwritten code of respect and openness to each other.

There are so many ways to reach the people you encounter on LinkedIn, such as accessing the contact information they provide in their profile, InMail, introductions, and messages to OpenLink members. It should be no problem to reach anyone in your network if you really want to meet that person.

Contacting Groups of People

Up until this point, we've been talking about finding someone and sending him or her a targeted message. As we say in marketing, it's the "rifle" approach. What if you want to use the "shotgun" approach and send the same message to many people on LinkedIn?

Before you do, you should be aware that any mass promotions in any medium—be it direct mail postcards, emails, or mass messages of any kind—have a low return rate. You're very lucky to get a 1 percent response rate from any kind of campaign of this nature. However, it's an accepted strategy in marketing and can be useful to you as long as you have realistic expectations.

The other consideration is that, in its infinite wisdom, LinkedIn has put in some controls over how many mass messages you can send in the system. Think about it: I have 23 million people in my network (that's first, second, and third levels). If I and other people were allowed to message millions of people every day with a push of a button, well, pretty soon the site would become overrun with mass mailings and turn into a swampy and spammy mess.

So, LinkedIn allows you to send mass messages but limits you to contacting 50 first-level connections at a time. To do so, click on *Contacts > Connections* to see your first-level connections. Sort them by location, companies, or industries, then click on the box next to each of their names and select 50 at a time. To the right you will see *Send Message*. Click on it and you will be given a text box in which to send a message to up to 50 first-level contacts (see Figure 8-5).

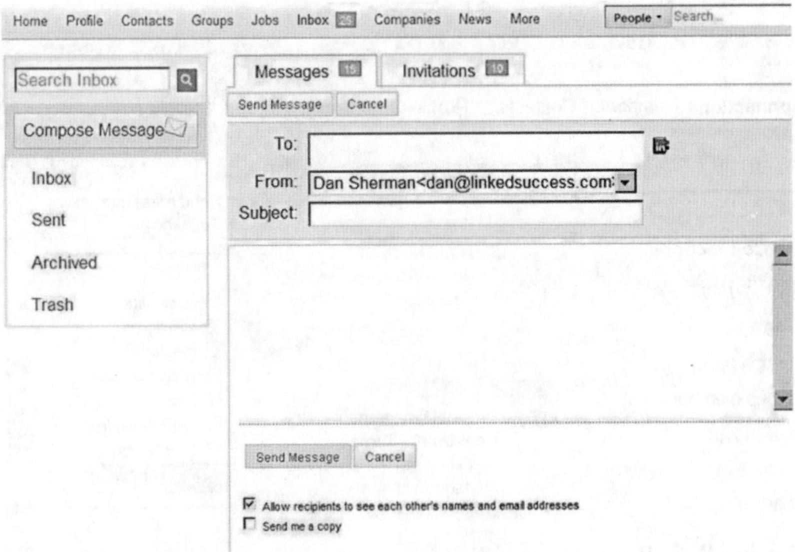

Figure 8-5. The Compose Message form allows you to send a message to up to 50 of your first-level connections. You can add contacts right from the form by clicking on the blue "in" box on the right, which will bring up all your contacts. Be sure to unclick the box below that allows recipients to see others' information to keep the message more professional.

Here's an important tip: before you click on the blue *Send Message* button, unclick the box that says *Allow recipients to see each other's names and email addresses*, so your contacts don't get upset that their personal information is being shared, and your message looks more targeted and professional.

Tag, You're It—Grouping Contacts

What if you want to send messages to the same group of people over and over again? There is a feature in My Connections called Tags that allows this. To create a group using Tags, go to *Contacts > Connections*, view your connections, and check off the people you want to tag into a group. Click the checkbox next to each name and you will see an *Edit tags* hyperlink appear on the right (see Figure 8-6). Click on it and a box will open where you can give this list of up to 50 people a group name, such as Atlanta Sales Managers or Miami Contacts; then push *Save*. The tagged group will then appear along the left-hand side of the page.

Figure 8-6. By clicking on *Edit tags* on the right, you can save 50 contacts into one group, which will help you organize your contacts for ongoing communications. Enter a name for the group and click *Save*. The groups you saved appear on the left under "Tags."

When you want to send a message to this tagged group, just click on the group tag name on the left-hand column and open up the tagged group. Across the top you will see *Select: All, None.* Click *All,* and then on the right side click *>Send Message.* That will pull up a text box where you can enter your message. Remember to deselect the check box next to where it says *Allow recipients to see each other's names and email addresses* on the bottom to protect the privacy of your contacts.

This method will allow you to group prospects, current customers, prospects by city, friends by city, or whatever you decide, and send a group message. Say you are traveling to Seattle on business. You can tag 50 Seattle prospects in a group and message them all at once, saying you are visiting and would like set up a time to grab coffee. Or you could put your top 50 clients in a group and message them all at once with a special, an open house, a new product announcement, and so on.

There is no limit to the number of tagged groups you can create, but you can send only 50 messages at a time. So if you have 100 Seattle prospects, for example, you can tag two groups; just call the first *Seattle prospects one* and the next *Seattle prospects two.*

Messaging More than 50 People

If you really want to send a message to more than 50 people, there is a way to do that, but you need to have an email management program. First, go to *Contacts > Connections,* look at the very bottom, and click on the link in the bottom right that says *Export Connections.* You can use this hyperlink to download all of your first-level connections to a CSV (comma-separated values) file.

Click on it, and on the next screen you will see your options for the type of CSV file you download. Then press the blue button that says *Export* and you will get an Excel spreadsheet with your contacts listed with their first and last names and email addresses. You can upload the contacts to an email management program and send out a mass email.

Finding a Mentor on LinkedIn

Going back to our earlier discussion on the many different types of helpful contacts you can make on LinkedIn, did you ever consider using the site to find a mentor?

You know the old saying, "Don't reinvent the wheel," right? Well, whatever you are working on, whatever projects or businesses you are striving to perfect, chances are good that someone out there has traveled the same road as you and can shed light on the process. Why wander around the forest without a flashlight when someone who has succeeded in your field can light a path for you?

Finding a mentor can cut your learning curve and let you achieve great results faster. And with over 175 million professionals on Linked-In, your potential pool for a good mentor is really substantial. So, how do you identify someone to help you find your way?

I used LinkedIn to contact a true expert on mentoring, Judy Hojel of Sydney, Australia, and asked her to provide her top 10 tips for finding a mentor on LinkedIn. Judy has a master's degree in education, and she is a professional speaker, writer, and business coach who has mentored hundreds of people, both those in the corporate world and those with their own businesses. She's an experienced CEO who specializes in leadership development and business growth.

Whether you are actively looking for a mentor, unsure of whether you want one, or pretty sure you don't need one, I still encourage you to read Judy's tips. What she says is excellent advice that applies to meeting anyone you want to connect with on LinkedIn to further your professional goals.

Here are Judy's top 10 tips:

A great mentor inspires you, teaches you, introduces you to new ways of thinking, pushes you out of your comfort zone, supports you in your business or career plans, and often acts as a sounding board. Finding a mentor can be a challenging and time-consuming process, although if you're on LinkedIn you're already ahead. Here are 10 smart tips that will speed up the search for your ideal mentor on LinkedIn.

1. **Be Clear About Your Mentoring Needs**

   This may sound obvious, but you need to be very clear about what you want from a mentor.

   Identify your expectations and needs.

   - Is the mentor to help move your career, business, or brand forward?
   - Do you need support and advice from someone who has been there and done that?
   - Do you need strategies for meeting your sales and profit targets?
   - Are you restructuring your business for growth?
   - Do you need fresh ideas or a different perspective on your everyday challenges?

   Remember too that you can have multiple mentors using LinkedIn, who can each help with specific situations and issues.

   When you have made a list of what you want help with, try an Advanced People Search using keywords for the type of mentor you are looking for. Just as Dan has instructed you to optimize your profile with the keywords you want to be found for, so too will your mentors have profiles full of the fields and specialities keywords that you need help with.

   Make a list of the people whose profiles are displayed, read their profiles to learn more about them, and look for ways to contact them. You now have a starting point and a list with which to begin your mentor search.

2. **Ask Your Own Network for Recommendations**

   Expand your search for referrals by reaching out to your own LinkedIn network and contacts. Ask who they use or who they might recommend from their own experience and why they would do so. If the person sounds promising, you can learn more about him by studying his LinkedIn profile and determining your best method of approach.

3. **Grow Your LinkedIn Network**

   In general, my advice is to connect with as many people as you can. This will help enormously in your search for a mentor on LinkedIn. Connect with business contacts at all levels of an organisation as well as those who own their own business. You benefit from having an expanded network, but you also benefit by being exposed to quality connections from your network. Don't forget to get to know the people in your LinkedIn network—you need to stand out and be memorable in their minds.

4. **Join Work-Related Groups**

   Join and participate in the LinkedIn Groups that match your needs. There are over a million special interest groups on LinkedIn, and current rules permit you to join up to 50. You can search for them by keywords or you can note the groups to which your potential mentors belong. Your old college might have an Alumni Group, as might your previous companies; both are useful hunting grounds for recommendations for mentors.

   Join up, watch the activity, and see who offers good, sound advice that resonates with you. Contribute to the discussions yourself; you never know where an exchange may lead in the search for your mentor.

5. **Ask a Question on the Q&A Forums**

   Consider asking a couple of those difficult questions you would put to your mentor on the LinkedIn Q&A forum. LinkedIn allows you 10 questions each month. There are many people who give their time and expertise to help others, and not only do you benefit from their knowledge, you have the opportunity to build more connections.

   Reply personally to everyone who answered your question and be prepared to share a little of yourself and your thinking in your email response to them. Many great email conversations begin by saying,

"Thanks so much for responding," which may turn out to be the perfect starting point to trust, respect, and rapport—the basics of a strong mentoring relationship.

Don't forget LinkedIn etiquette—remember to close the question and rate the answers.

6. **Read the Answers on the Q&A Forums**

LinkedIn has many categories on the Q&A Forums where people can post and answer questions. There's even one for *Mentoring* under the category of *Careers and Education*. Choose two or three categories that interest you and observe who is contributing valuable information to the discussion.

Who gets excited about participating and whose responses help you see things with greater clarity? Whose guidance or style appeals to you? These people will probably make a great mentor, so get to know them. Check out their profile, read their previous answers, connect with them, develop a dialogue, and see where it leads.

7. **Watch the Events Your Network Is Attending**

LinkedIn offers a great feature where organisers are able to promote a LinkedIn Event, whether it is a breakfast briefing or after-work networking and drinks. You then get notified directly if you are part of that group, or indirectly if someone in your network has clicked to say they are interested or will be attending.

Should you be there? Absolutely! Attending a professional event is a great place to continue your search for a mentor or to determine your compatibility with a couple of people you may have already identified.

Contact them through LinkedIn to say you will be attending and how much you look forward to meeting them. Having face-to-face contact is often the best way to tell whether you really connect well together. If you do, approach them about becoming a mentor or arrange another time where you can talk more freely.

8. **Turn Good Connections into Good Relationships**

   Numbers aren't everything on LinkedIn! Social networking is all about building relationships. Think about how you can help others as much as you are wanting help yourself. Build a quality network and become memorable by sharing articles, contributing your expertise, participating in discussions, liking posts, and commenting positively on information shared from your network. Remember you want to be the type of person that others would be excited to mentor, so put effort into building good relationships.

   Remember too that not every one of your mentors needs to live close by, so don't discount those terrific people in other countries. Instead, recognise that they may be ideal to help with specific situations and problems you are dealing with.

9. **Think Creatively About Finding a Mentor**

   There are some people that you would love as a mentor, but you are worried that they might be too busy or too high-ranking to mentor you. The only way to find out is to be a little creative in how you approach them.

   Use the connection you have developed through LinkedIn to invite them to speak at a work event or ask them to submit an article for your company newsletter. Most independent professionals are always glad to get work, and this may be a great way to get to know them on a face-to-face basis. If they say no, thank them for their time and consideration. After all, every no gets you a step further to "yes, I'd love to talk about mentoring with you"!

10. **Keep Your LinkedIn Profile Up to Date**

    Your LinkedIn Profile showcases you to potential mentors. When you start building relationships, you'll find people heading over to your profile to learn more about you, and it's important that their impression is favorable! Invest time in building your brand and you'll find that potential mentors are more willing to invest time in you.

Next Steps

There is no reason to keep the mentoring relationship online if you find it has gone to the next level. Many people prefer a face-to-face conversation, while others remain happy with phone calls and emails. It really depends on what suits both your needs, but as with everything worthwhile it will take some work to get it just right.

The right mentor can make all the difference to your career, your job satisfaction, and your earning capacity. With so many professionals on LinkedIn and so many ways to find the right mentor, the search process has never been easier!

You can find out more about Judy's company at http://au.linkedin.com/in/judyhojel.

Final Thoughts on Mentors: Work at the Relationship

Putting into place Judy's great tips is really the start of the process. I'll just add that mentoring requires a time investment on the part of the professional you want to work with and get help from, so work on building a relationship first before you ask for mentoring. If you ask someone you don't know to help you with mentoring, you may not succeed. But if you get to know that person over time by conversing with him, following his activity on LinkedIn, and talking in person during an event you both attend, you stand a much better chance.

* * *

Searching for people and contacting them on LinkedIn is easy. Get active on the site and start networking, and soon you will have many people you want to reach. When you message them directly, be respectful and tactful and remember that people want to feel unique. What is it about them specifically that made you want to reach out? As long as you are honest and precise, you will find other LinkedIn users open to hearing from you.

What's another great way to expand your network of potential customers, partners, mentors, and advisors? The answer is in the herd—namely, LinkedIn Groups. Follow along as we take a look at one of the most powerful features on the site.

Chapter 9: Power in Tribes: Joining and Creating Groups

You've heard the saying "birds of a feather flock together"? That old adage definitely applies to LinkedIn. The millions of professionals who joined the site have aligned themselves into a dizzying array of combinations: there are corporation groups, alumni groups, nonprofit groups, professional groups, networking groups, city groups—a million of them in every language under the sun from Croatian to Slovak to Chinese to Polish. There are also groups to help you become better at LinkedIn (not-so-subtle plug: I own one called Link Success with Dan Sherman).

What that means for you is an incredible opportunity for prospecting and finding exactly the right person you want to meet to achieve your goals—be it selling a product, finding a partner, hiring someone, finding a job, and so on. The people you need to find are all waiting there for you in groups, and you can join up to 50 groups at a time and begin the networking that will lead you to getting to know and contacting the people you want to meet.

Groups are great for building your brand. You can answer people's questions and post articles of interest for group members to read. This establishes you as an expert, so it's a great way to be found on LinkedIn by people who may need your services and wish to hire you. Groups will also help your offline marketing: you can learn about upcoming networking events that might benefit your career or business, and you can promote your events to like-minded individuals. You can search for jobs (every group has a job board) and contact fellow group members even if they are not first-, second-, or third-level connections.

What's helpful is that as your interests and goals change over time, so can your group lineup. It's a snap to leave one group (no one is notified and there's no shame involved) and join another that fits your current needs. And groups drastically extend your reach. Yes, you should be adding first-level contacts daily, but additionally, by joining 50 groups with 1,000 potential customers in each group, you just added 50,000 prospects you can now network with and contact in order to conduct business together.

Joining Groups

Across the top menu bar, click on *Groups* > *Group Directory*. There is a *Search Groups* feature offering three sorting criteria (see Figure 9-1). In the first box, you can add a keyword for the kind of subject matter you want your potential group to be about. In the next box is a drop-down menu where you can specify the type of group you are looking for (corporate, alumni, networking, nonprofit, professional, and so on.) In the third box, select from the drop-down menu any of 45 different languages for the group you wish to join.

Now, type in a keyword and look for groups you can join that match your interest. You'll be tempted to join groups of your peers, and that's a great idea. Join a few industry groups in the field in which you are involved so that you can stay up to date on the very latest events and trends.

For example, I teach social media, which is a field that changes minute by minute. So I find that by being in the largest social media groups, I have access to what the thought leaders are saying and how the landscape is shifting. Look for the largest groups in your field, and join the discussions.

Another benefit of joining groups in your industry is that all the groups are displayed on your profile, and everything counts toward searchability and credibility. So I have joined many social media groups and LinkedIn groups not only to learn, but also to have group titles appear on my profile. They are terms I want to be found for,

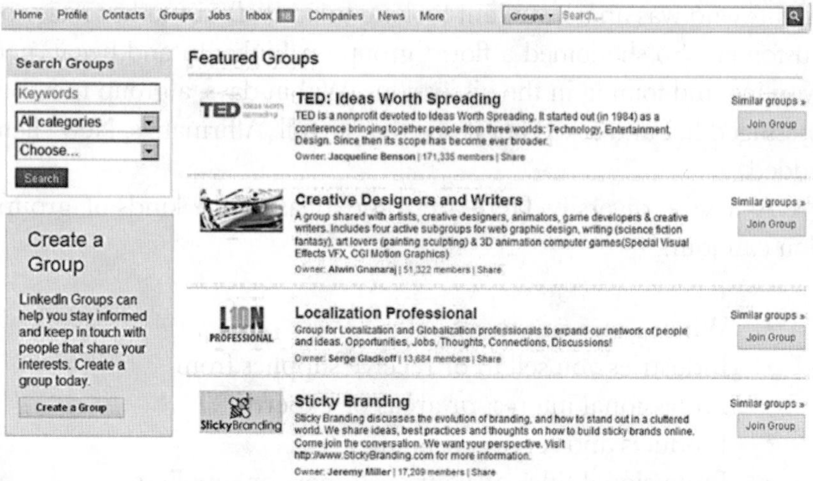

Figure 9-1. On the Groups search page, you can enter keywords and find groups that match your interest. You can join them on this page by clicking on the *Join Group* button on the right or find similar groups by clicking on the *Similar groups* hyperlink. You can also start a group from this page by clicking on the *Create a Group* button on the left.

and they show readers of my profile that I'm keeping current with trends in my industry. Having social media groups in my profile serves to create consistency in my brand: I teach social media, and I network with other social media enthusiasts and thought leaders.

The next thing you might do is join your local groups. Type the name of your city in the keyword search box and see what groups are the largest. I am in a half dozen groups in my town because even though online networking rocks, in-person contact is still critical to meeting referral partners and finding customers for my services and local training events. My local groups keep me informed of upcoming networking and social events right in my backyard.

Diversify Your Groups

When it comes to groups, diversify! One of the key strategies to undertake is to join not only your industry and alumni groups, but also groups where your customers are likely to be. I gave this advice to one of my clients who was an accountant looking to add a florist to her roster of customers. So she joined a florist group on LinkedIn and began networking and joining in the discussions. Within days, a group member messaged her and asked her if she did payroll. Affirmative. New client added.

As I said, diversify. Here are some ideas of the kinds of groups you can join:

- Where you went to school
- Industries you sell to or receive supplies from
- Professional interest or areas of expertise
- Products and services you offer
- Professional titles of your customers or suppliers
- Clubs and associations
- Companies you worked for in the past
- Nonprofits and hobbies you are interested in

Most important of all: join groups where your clients are going to be congregating. In the Group Search area, put the keyword or title for your best prospects. If you sell to human resources executives, then add that keyword and click the blue *Search* button. When a list of potential groups appears, click on the title of the group you want to explore, then check out some discussions and find groups that are active; there are discussions added every day. Then make the leap: click on the blue button that says *Join Group*. Remember, it's easy to switch in and out, so there's really no pressure. Some groups are auto-accept (meaning that by clicking *Join Group*, immediately you are in). For other groups, the group manager will look you over a bit before agreeing to accept you. In the six years I've been on LinkedIn, there were maybe one or two that never approved me, but there are so many groups to join that overlap in content that it's not an issue if one doesn't accept me. I just move on to the next group and apply.

When it comes to joining groups, size matters. Once you put in your keyword, the groups will appear ranked by number of members. It's always a good idea to join the largest groups so you have exposure to more people and can make the most connections. Join the largest groups in your region and you can network with lots of people right in your own backyard. Also, try combinations of words to see if you can locate the perfect group for your purpose. Include a region and a field, such as *New York Doctors* or *Phoenix Social Media.* You don't need quotes or Boolean search terms (such as *And* or *Not*); LinkedIn will search the group profiles and return groups that contain those words in the profile.

You can research a group you are interested in joining by clicking on the box that says *Group Statistics* along the right-hand side close to the bottom of the group's page. That will open up a screen that will show you interesting facts about the group, including how many members have joined, where they are located, what their job titles are, how fast the group is growing, and how much activity the group is experiencing.

Here's another strategy for selecting groups: as you join in conversations on LinkedIn and find an interesting person, such as a prospective partner, customer, advisor, or competitor, look at the person's profile and see which groups she belongs to by scrolling down to the end of her page. You may make some interesting discoveries and find groups that will benefit you, and you can join the groups right from that person's profile. There is a *+Join* right under the name of any group you have not joined yet. This comes in handy if you want to message a person and she is not a first-level connection; just join a group that person is in and you have that ability.

Navigating Your Groups

Once you join a group after locating it using a keyword search or seeing it on someone's profile, you'll see a toolbar across the top within the group (see Figure 9-2). The first tab is *Discussions.* There is where everyone is talking about the group topic. To join a discussion, just click on a headline of a post and you will see a space to add your comment. By commenting on discussions and adding relevant, helpful information, you increase your presence in the group and reinforce your brand. When people see what you wrote, they can click on your picture, read your profile, and contact you for further discussions on how you can work together.

What else can you do in the Discussions area? Underneath each discussion post, you have a list of options. You can do the following:

- You can "like it," which puts your smiling face on the discussion page. That helps to increase awareness of your brand. It also updates your status, meaning that all your first-level connections also see your action on their home pages.
- You can comment and open the possibility of someone connecting with you because of what you said.
- You can follow the discussion and get email updates on the thread.
- You can click *Flag* to mark the post for the attention of the group manager.
- You can click on *More,* which opens up a drop-down menu with two choices: you can click on *Share Link* and you will be able to send the discussion to other groups or other LinkedIn members (thus establishing you as a helpful thought leader on the site), or you can click on *Reply Privately* to open up a text box where you can initiate a conversation directly with the posting member. That enables you to connect with those who are open to assistance from you or who may be in a position to assist you with your goals.

The next tab on a group page is *Members*; click on that and you will see all the members in the group sorted by the ones closest to you (first level, then second level, etc.) This will show you people with whom you might want to connect. There's even a keyword search for members. In the upper left of the page, it says *Search members*; there you can put in a title, a city, or anything to sort the members. For example, I'm in the Branded Entertainment group with over 4,000 members. If I put my city, Tampa, in the search box, I get 17 members; these are local people interested in a topic I find fascinating, namely product placement, with whom I can connect.

The next tab is *Promotions*, where posts go that are promoting something and the manager feels they do not fit in the Discussions area. The next tab is *Jobs*, where you will see paid job postings. Also in this section are the job postings added for free by the group members; over on the left, click on the hyperlink *Job Discussions* to reach those listings. There is a *Search* tab for finding discussions by keyword. The last tab, *More*, is where you click on *My settings* to adjust how often and in what manner the group members and manager can message you.

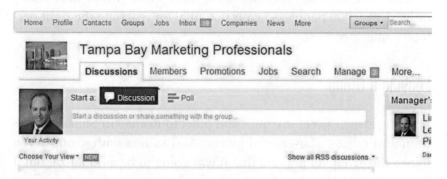

Figure 9-2. The tabs across the top within the groups give you access to much information, including who the members are, what jobs are being posted, and how you can control your group settings.

When you find a group you like, one strategy that is helpful is to message the group manager and offer to connect with him (i.e., become a first-level connection). If he has started and manages a very large group in an area of interest to you, he would be someone good to know. Within the group, click on *More > Group Profile* and look for the *About this Group* on the right. There you will see the group manager's name as a hyperlink to his profile. Review the profile and send a message to him introducing yourself and offering to be a moderator or anything else you can do to help, such as helping to organize local meetings.

Messaging Group Members

One powerful reason for joining many groups is that you can message people directly even if you are not a first-level connection and without spending money on an InMail. So if there is someone you want to connect with, say a second- or third-level connection, within the group, go to *Members* and highlight the person by hovering your mouse over her name. You will see on the right-hand side two hyper-linked choices: *Invite to connect* and *Send message*. Click on *Send message* and a text box will open for your message. If you join 50 groups with 1,000 prospects each, that's 50,000 more people you can message and look for ways to do business together. Most groups have many more than 1,000 people, so your potential for reaching the right person is unlimited.

Leaving a Group

"Parting is such sweet sorrow," said Juliet to Romeo in Shakespeare's immortal tale of star-crossed lovers. And so it is with groups. You joined the group all hopeful that it was going to be a bonanza, but it became a dud. You therefore have mixed emotions about the group. Should you stay, or should you go? If you decide to leave, no problem. You can leave any time simply by going to the group page; on the top menu in the group, click on *More > Your Settings* and find the *Leave Group* button in the lower right. Click on it, and you are automatically out of the group.

As a group manager, I can tell you there is no stigma involved; no one knows but you. No one is notified. So you can shuffle around your 50 allotted groups as often as you like to suit your present needs, and no one is the wiser.

So you can see that groups open up a whole range of possibilities for you in terms of learning new things, meeting new people, connecting with prospects, and establishing your brand. But just like they say on TV: *But Wait! There's More!* You can start your own group and build a perpetual prospecting machine.

Creating a Group

You've heard about the Golden Rule? The one that says, "Those who have the gold make the rules"? Well, LinkedIn offers you the chance to have the gold and the control, be the big kahuna, and make all the rules. All you need to do is start your own group, and you can create up to 10 of them. Once you do, you are in a position to establish yourself as a thought leader, gain credibility, be found for opportunities, and expand your networking capabilities. Also, and very importantly, you can use group management automation features to create a system that delivers prospects and website traffic to your door around the clock so you get leads while you sleep.

To get started, come up with an idea for a group—perhaps a group for your industry, a group that combines locale and industry, or a group for a passion of yours. You might make a group where your potential customers can congregate. Say you sell computer equipment; you'd want to start a group for IT professionals. If you sell sales training, start a group for VPs of Sales. Whatever your expertise is, whatever product you sell, you can begin a group in that field and begin networking with prospective clients. One strategy is to create a local group for your customers that allows you to meet people and then move conversations offline. So if you sell to sales managers, instead of a sales managers' group, you create "Portland Sales Managers" or whatever your locale is.

To begin the process, first click on *Groups* on the top menu, then click *Create a Group*. You will see a very simple form you can fill out in two minutes and begin promoting your group right away. Here is what you will need to add:

- **Logo.** This should be something clean and professional. More people will join if you have a logo rather than the default LinkedIn image. Just find a royalty-free image from the web.
- **Group Name.** This can be as long as you want, but you should use up to four words that create a concise message of what your group is about. Keep in mind when creating your name that it will be searchable in the keyword search on LinkedIn. So make sure it contains the keyword that you feel your potential group members will be typing in to find groups to join.

- **Group Type.** You have several choices here, including professional, networking, corporate, and so on. Pick the one that best applies to your purpose.
- **Summary.** This should be a benefit-oriented statement: What is it that people will gain from joining your group? What's in it for them?
- **Description.** Elaborate on the benefits of your group and add in details about what people should talk about, whether this group will be online only or will include offline events, and how to reach you if they have questions. Include keywords that you think people will use to find the group, since that's where LinkedIn looks when someone does a search.
- **Group Owner Email.** Include an email address that you check often in case someone writes to you with an opportunity.
- **Website.** Put the address of your company website or blog here so that you can drive traffic to your site from your group.
- **Access.** There are some settings you need to select to finish the process. One is to select *Auto join* or *Request to join*. With *Auto join*, whoever applies is accepted immediately while *Request to join* means you have to approve them. In my experience, the *Request to join* option is too much work, since you need to approve everybody. I now use *Auto join* and let whomever wants to join my groups do so—it's easy to remove them if you need to later. However, if you are starting a group for only a very select cross section of people—say, your premium clients, or those with a certain degree or background—then use the *Request to join* option to screen applicants.
- **Open or Members-Only Group.** At the end of this form, you will be asked if you want this to be an Open or Members-Only group. If you are creating the group to be a traffic generator, definitely choose *Open*, as the discussions can be seen by anyone on LinkedIn and searched for on Google as well. Also, in an open group, people who aren't members can still add discussions from anywhere in the LinkedIn network, which encourages more interaction.

Promoting Your Group

Once you create your group, it will have its own unique URL. The link is pretty long and ugly; to send it to others, you can go to a free URL shortening site like Bit.ly or Tinyurl.com to create a smaller link. Once you've done that, here are some ideas on how to promote your group:

- Send the URL via email to any contacts who may be interested in joining such a group.
- Add the URL to your email signature.
- Add it to your LinkedIn status update on a regular basis, inviting your first-level connections to join your group. (Your status update appears on all your first-level connections' home pages.) I put the link to join my group, Link Success with Dan Sherman, in my status update about once a week.

To actively promote your group, go to your group, click on *Manage*, and you will have a wide array of methods for reaching potential group members. Here you can:

- **Send Invitations.** This option allows you to invite your first-level contacts to join your group. Click on it, and you will see the invitation form. You will see the blue "in" logo next to the box marked *Connections*. Click on it, and you will see all your first-level connections. You can click on 50 people at a time and invite them to join your group. If you are creating a local group, then select connections in that locale. If you are creating an industry group, sort by industry. Then, erase the canned LinkedIn welcome message that asks people to join. Compose your own personal message that explains why you started the group, what the purpose is, and how it will benefit people to join it, and then send your invites.
- **Group Link.** Click on *Send Invitations* to get to the invitation screen, and you will see *Group Join Link* on the lower left. This URL hyperlinks right to your LinkedIn group page. Copy and paste that into your status updates and posts on other

social media sites like Facebook and Twitter; put the link on your website, in your email signature, and on your LinkedIn Profile. This will provide a wider exposure for your group, and you'll get more members as a result.

Over time, your group will slowly build. One great feature of LinkedIn that will help you is that when someone joins your group, that fact appears in that person's status updates, which also appears on all their first-level contacts' pages. When a friend of your contact sees that she has joined your new group, he may be inspired to join as well if he is interested in the subject.

Creating Subgroups for More Influence

When you click on *Manage* in your group, way down on the bottom of the left-hand menu is *Subgroups*. This feature extends your ability to create groups, because you can have 10 subgroups for each of the 10 allowed groups you can create. Let's say you create a group around a passion, say start-ups, where you talk about building the next Google or Apple. You could create subgroups for different locations around the country, such as "Start-ups Denver" or "Start-ups Houston," which will enable you to create and send targeted messages to people if you're planning an event in that city.

Subgroups give you the ability to extend your influence and also create highly targeted groups of professionals. You can send a different message to each subgroup that promotes different things or discusses different aspects of your group topic. The process for creating a subgroup is identical to that for creating a group; it's just a part of your larger group.

Subgroups give you flexibility. Let's say you want your main group to be open and automatically accept everyone. You could make the subgroups more selective so you would have to approve everyone who wanted to be in those groups.

Building Your Business with a Group

Once you have your groups established, you can use them to not only build your personal brand but also build your lists of prospects through automation. Here is what I do with my groups. I maintain two groups on LinkedIn. The first is Tampa Bay Marketing Professionals, with over 3,700 members; this group is for professionals in sales, marketing, advertising, and public relations to network and share opportunities. Even though it says Tampa Bay, I get people from all over the world joining, which is fine—it increases my exposure. This group helps my personal brand immensely as an Internet professional and social media expert.

My second group is Link Success with Dan Sherman, which I created to provide a place for conversations around achieving professional goals by using LinkedIn. This group also gives me the opportunity to brand myself as a LinkedIn and social media expert.

So how do these groups help me create my brand and pull more opportunities to me as a LinkedIn expert? Let's look at some ways.

Manager's Choice

When you start a group, one of the areas over which you have total control is the main part of the group, the discussion area. You can select what discussions appear on the site, and you can choose to not accept other discussions. To set up how you want your group discussion selection to run, go to your group, click on *Manage*, then click on *Group Settings* on the left. Under *Permissions,* you can choose to have everything submitted to you for approval, or you can set it to where everyone's discussion posts appears automatically.

In my two groups, I set up Tampa Bay Marketing Professionals so that all discussions submitted are automatically posted, because it is a pretty diverse group in terms of membership and interest. (I still have the option to either delete inappropriate discussions or move them to other areas.) In Link Success with Dan Sherman, I set it up so that I need to approve all discussions, since this is a very niche group that is only about LinkedIn, and I want tighter control.

In both groups, I can make any discussion I want to be the most prominent by selecting it as *Manager's Choice*. It then appears in the upper right of the group home page, so it's the first thing people see when they come to the group. I use that space as a mini-billboard for anything I am promoting at the moment. It's easy to make a discussion in your group a Manager's Choice; just click on the discussion headline, open it up, and click the hyperlinked *Manager's Choice* right above the discussion.

Announcements

As group manager, I can send an announcement every seven days to my group members that gets delivered to their regular email inboxes. I use this quite a bit with my Tampa group to announce upcoming local LinkedIn trainings I'm going to be doing. In the message, I write a catchy subject line and include a link to an online invitation to come to my training. (I use Eventbrite.com for many of my trainings, which is an event-organizing and fee-collection website with a robust set of management features.) So I have a 3,700-strong, targeted email list of people I can mail to. I get about five people a day signing up to my group, so my email list grows organically. The larger you can make your group, the more people you can reach with your announcements.

To make an announcement, go to *Manage* in your group and select *Send an announcement* from the left-hand menu.

Templates

I have completely automated both of my groups with marketing messages that go out to any LinkedIn professional who wants to join. What these messages do is introduce me and promote what I can do personally for them. They also provide all my websites, products, and resources, and they tell people how they can contact me to further the relationship.

These messages are fully automated and work 24/7 for me, promoting my LinkedIn trainings and helping to build my brand with people from around the world who join my groups. Let's see what the two messages look like.

Here's what LinkedIn users get in their email box when they apply to my Tampa group. You can see that I'm branding myself and giving them my URL where they can learn more about me:

Thank you for applying to the Tampa Bay Marketing
Professionals Group. I'm Dan Sherman, Group Manager, and
I approve your application!
Dan Sherman, LinkedIn Expert, Social Media Coach,
Trainer, Author, and Speaker
http://www.LinkedSuccess.com

I have this group set to auto-accept everyone. Once they are automatically accepted into the group, they get this message in their Gmail or Hotmail account, or whatever email program they are using:

Do you want to grow your business? Learn advanced
LinkedIn techniques with a consultation or seminar with
Dan Sherman, LinkedIn expert. Call 813. . . or email dan@
linkedsuccess.com.
Welcome to our group of professionals in all areas of
marketing, sales, public relations, and advertising. As group
manager, I encourage you to actively participate by asking
questions, offering advice, and letting everyone know about
upcoming events related to our profession.
I am an open networker, meaning I accept all invitations
to connect. Please send me an invitation to connect with you.
Again, welcome, and let me know how I can assist you in
achieving your business goals with LinkedIn.
Dan Sherman/LinkedIn Expert
http://www.linkedsuccess.com
dan@linkedsuccess.com

Here you can see I'm promoting my LinkedIn training; I'm branding myself as an expert; I'm providing a URL to my main site, where they can read more about me; I'm inviting them to connect with me so I build my sphere of influence; and I provide my email address and phone number so they can contact me.

These templates are a snap to set up. You just go to your group, click *Manage* from the top toolbar, select *Templates* from the left-hand menu, and then notice the *Manage Message Templates* screen, where you create your automated messages to go out to people who apply to join and who are accepted. (See Figure 9-3.) You have the option to also send yourself a test message from this screen so you can see how your message looks in your inbox. If you include URLs, be sure to add the *http://* so they come out as hyperlinks.

Figure 9-3. The Manage Group section gives you a wide variety of tools for managing your group and many communications methods for establishing your personal brand.

Imagine what you can do with this ability:

- You can create a free offer.
- You can drive new members to a place to sign up for your newsletter.
- You can drive people to a website where you can capture their email addresses in exchange for a free report.
- You can sell a course or promote an event.
- You can provide a way for them to reach you or connect with you on other social media sites.

The possibilities are endless, and they are automated so you can grow your email list and make sales while you sleep.

A Wise Name and Logo Choice

Here's another creative way I use groups to strengthen my personal brand and create more visibility for myself. It's by the use of my name and a very clever logo for my group, Link Success with Dan Sherman. You can see I'm branding myself with the name of the group by associating my name (my brand) with Link Success. (Due to copyright restrictions, LinkedIn does not allow anyone to use its company name in a group title.)

The logo is my brand, too. Log onto LinkedIn, go to *Groups > Group Directory*, and search for my group, Link Success with Dan Sherman. Then join! Trust me, you'll like the group. Now the group is going to show up in your list of groups on your profile. If you look at the logo for the group, you'll discover my smiling face. Yes, I am the logo for Link Success.

What this means is that I'm branding myself with my face on *your* profile and every person's profile who joins the group. And my face (which is part of my brand as a speaker) shows up next to the words *Link Success with Dan Sherman*, which anyone can interpret as success with LinkedIn. Now anyone scanning your profile or another of our group members' profile gets a brand reinforcement of me as the LinkedIn expert. So the more people who join the group, the larger my brand grows on LinkedIn.

This is an example of how you can get very creative with groups to establish yourself as a thought leader in your field and have others seek you out.

Getting Group Members Engaged

When you start a group, you need to assume leadership and pro-actively start conversations, post timely news, and react quickly to the discussions and questions of others. This includes moderating discussions and removing distracting posts that are just total self-promotions and contribute nothing to your group. As your membership grows, discussions become self-generating, but it's important to check the engagement in your group and generate discussions regularly.

One tactic you may want to try is sharing worthy posts you see in other groups that your members would enjoy. It's easy to do, since every group post contains a share feature where you can select other groups in which to display it. Just click on *More* > *Share Link* under a post when you want to put that post from another group into yours. By clicking on the link, it brings up the Share box that allows you to post the discussion in your update, post it to groups, or send it to other connections on LinkedIn.

Another strategy is to read industry blogs and, when you see a post that would interest your group members, share it with your group. For example, I like sharing interesting articles I read about LinkedIn with my two groups. So I regularly read two of the most well-known social media blogs, Mashable and Tech Crunch. When I read an article I feel my group members would enjoy, I use the sharing features in the blogs and add them to my groups.

Building Website Traffic with Groups

As we leave our discussion on Groups, I want to share with you one more strategy that you can use to turn your group memberships into solid traffic for your blog. It's simple and easy to do.

Let's say you have a blog and you want more readers to visit it and get to know about your expertise and your products. Basically, every time you create a new blog post, add it as a discussion in a group where the members would enjoy the subject. Find the group where you want to publicize your blog post and go to *Start a discussion.* Describe what the post is about in the first box; next, in the *Add more details* area, provide more reasons why people should be interested; finally, click on the paperclip logo and *Attach a link* and attach a link that goes directly to the web page with the blog post.

Then, once the discussion has been posted, click on *More > Share Link* under the discussion post. This will bring up a *Share* box. Check the box next to the line that reads *Post to group(s).* That will open up a box where you will see *Groups.* Where it says *Start typing the name of the group,* begin by typing the letter *a,* then *b,* then *c,* and so on. LinkedIn will fill in the names of all the groups of which you are a member. Select the groups that are relevant to your blog post and add them; fill in *Subject* and *Detail,* then press the blue *Share* button. Your blog post will now appear simultaneously in all your groups with a link to your blog. Group members can click on it, read your blog post on your blog's site, and, if they are intrigued, they can stick around, read more posts, learn more about you, and perhaps sign up for a newsletter.

This will enable thousands of group members to visit your blog and learn more about what you have to offer. I would caution you in two ways: First, don't overuse this. Maybe apply this strategy once or twice a week so you don't inundate your groups. Second, make sure the blog post is relevant to the subject matter of the group. For example, putting a post about real estate into a group about medical trends would defeat the purpose.

* * *

So begin joining groups, interact with others, and contact the people with whom you want to do business. Then start your own groups to help you achieve your personal branding and professional goals. You will be amazed at the possibilities. In the next chapter, I am going to talk about an incredibly effective way to establish yourself as a worldwide expert and pull business to you: LinkedIn Answers.

Chapter 10: Give to Get: Answering and Asking Questions

LinkedIn is many things. First, it's a contact management system that surpasses anything on the market. I used to be an ACT! devotee. Comparing the two, LinkedIn is like one of the massive multiplayer online games and ACT! is like *Pong*.

Second, LinkedIn is a free site to post a multimedia lead-generating profile that engages your reader, sends out your content, and pulls targeted traffic to your site around the clock while you sleep.

Third, it's a gigantic custom-designed encyclopedia of knowledge where you can not only establish yourself as a worldwide thought leader, but also pull business toward you based on your wisdom *and* save on consulting fees. The place you do all that? LinkedIn Answers.

This important section is where you can publish knowledge in your field of expertise by answering questions. By putting yourself out there, you become a thought leader, and sales and media opportunities will start to flow your way. You can also ask questions, and that carries with it a significant benefit in terms of personal branding and saving lots of cash on consulting fees.

How to Answer Questions

Let's start with answering questions. Along the top toolbar, click on *More* > *Answers*. That takes you to the Answers Home page. The fifth tab, all the way on the right, is the *Answer Questions* tab. Click on it and browse the menu on the right of all the different areas where people are looking for your knowledge, from Financial Markets to Personal Finance, from Management to Technology (see Figure 10-1). All the headings in the column are hyperlinks, and when you click on one, LinkedIn displays questions from your network on that topic. All you do is click on a question and answer it!

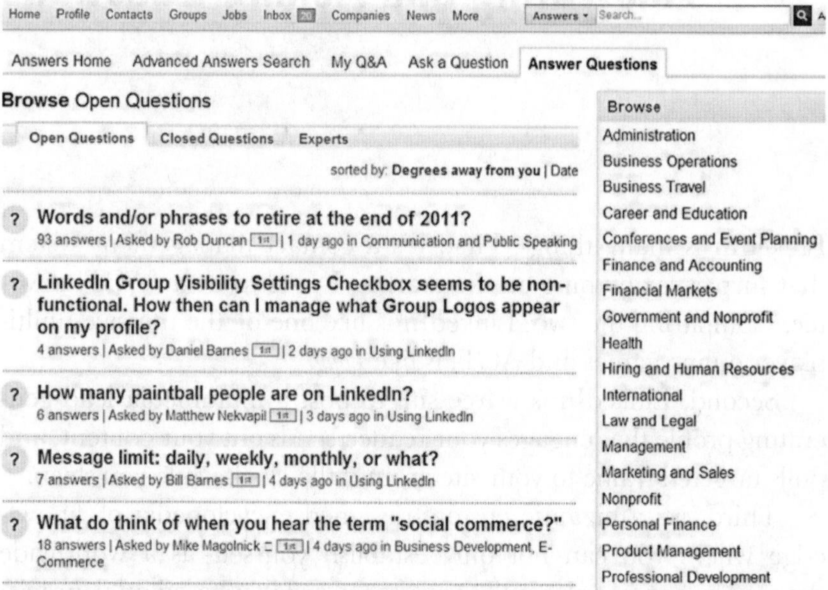

Figure 10-1. The Answer Questions tab displays open questions you can answer and a list of categories you can choose from along the right.

When you answer a question, your response is listed on that page along with your profile name and headline. That way, others who peruse the questions can read your sage advice, click on your name, and go right to your profile to find out more about what you do, giving you valuable exposure. The more questions you answer, the more visibility you get on LinkedIn and the better chance you have of people connecting with you (which expands your network of first-level connections) and also sending you business. I have heard of LinkedIn users getting thousands of dollars in consulting gigs just from taking the time to answer questions.

The more questions you answer, the more chance you also have to be rated an Expert on LinkedIn. When the question "closes" in seven days, the person asking the question has the chance to rate the answers. If you are selected as best answer, you will get a star near your name in the Answer section, and you will appear in a list of experts for that topic. Also, your expert status is noted on your profile. So, people searching for experts to hire on any professional topic listed on LinkedIn will find you if you have been providing value by answering questions and being rated as an expert.

Answering a question allows you to provide value to someone who needs expertise. If your answer is a good one, the person will click through to your profile and see who you are, perhaps downloading your articles and viewing your videos and then visiting your website. It's great publicity for you and perhaps one of best methods for getting your name out there.

You can even be more proactive than just answering the question. I know from years of experience as a marketer that I just love it when a prospect raises his hand and identifies himself as needing what I offer. It's easier to spot the people I can sell to as a result. When someone asks a question, he is saying that he needs help.

With that in mind, after you answer a question but before you submit your answer, LinkedIn provides you with a text box on the bottom that says, *Write a note to "name" (optional).* Here you have a chance to include a direct message to the person who asked a question that lands in his or her LinkedIn inbox.

Obviously, this person has a need, a pain, in an area where you are an expert. So you answer the question publicly *and* reply privately with some kind of offer. You might suggest that the person take advantage of any of the following, such as:

- A 15-minute free phone consultation
- A website where the person can watch a video you made on the topic
- A coaching program you run where the person can get help
- A book you wrote that provides more in-depth assistance
- A webinar you are conducting

In my case, I have made it a habit to spend 20 minutes each morning answering questions in my specialty topic, Using LinkedIn. This does a lot for me:

- It introduces me to people who are prospects for my book and my online trainings on LinkedIn.
- It has added to my network because many people I help on Answers send me an invitation to connect.
- It has introduced me to partners who check out my profile after I answer a question and write me asking to work together. I've been a guest on teleseminars and webinars teaching Linked-In strategies as a result, and this has exposed me to wider audiences who have bought my consulting services. It's also how I found mentoring expert Judy Hojel, whom you met in Chapter 8. Plus, you have no limits on your answers; you can answer as many questions as you like.

I answer questions as one of the ways I am establishing myself as a thought leader using LinkedIn while building my client and partner list. As a LinkedIn consultant, answering questions also provides me with great insight into what areas people have issues with so that I can build the answers into my writings and online trainings on LinkedIn. It's free market research; whatever field you're in, you can use Answers to discover what are the burning issues of the day in your area. It's something I work on every day (I answer at least five questions a day), and if you do too, gradually you will see results.

Asking Questions

As far as asking questions, you can ask up to 10 a month. I do it for two reasons: one, I save on consulting fees; two, I get free branding. Let's examine reason one first.

I don't know everything! Yes, it's startling to realize that, but it's true. By asking questions, I get the combined global wisdom of my 23 million strong network to help me for the unbelievably low price of zilch, zero, nada.

I have asked 100 questions on LinkedIn, and many of my questions are about technical issues in web building (such as HTML problems), which I just don't know because I'm not a code jockey. Or I ask for recommendations for software programs I need to run my business. So let's do the math. A typical consultant gets paid anywhere from $100 to $300 an hour. If I had to hire a consultant to answer these questions and I was charged $100 an hour, I would be out over $10,000. But I get more than one answer to each question, and I have paid nothing.

There's a fancy term for this: crowdsourcing. Basically, you tap into the wisdom of the crowd to achieve your goals. An entire industry has sprung up around the idea of using the Internet to crowdsource services and solutions, and there are crowdsourcing websites in every field, notably graphic design (one of the best examples is www.99designs.com). Some cost money; some don't. LinkedIn Answers is like free crowdsourcing.

Therefore, asking questions enables me to save money on consulting fees. And since LinkedIn stores all the questions I asked along with the answers, I can go back any time and reference them. It's like having my own personalized encyclopedia of information created just for me by experts from around the world. I encourage you to tap into your network next time you get stuck. You get fast, free answers that will get you moving in no time.

How to Ask Questions

How do you ask a question? When you click on *More* on the top bar and you click on *Answers*, you will wind up on the Answers Home page (see Figure 10-2). The first thing you see is a text box where you can ask a question. That text box is for the headline of your question, not the whole thing. Just summarize your question and put what it's about. Then click the blue *Next* button.

What you will see then is a list of similar questions that were asked previously, which you can reference. This is good if you are really in a hurry and you just want to find the answer fast. If you are not in a rush, just ignore that list and go to the *Add details* section, where you write out the entire question. Provide as much detail as you can so that you get the best possible answers. It goes without saying that your question should be typo free and written with the correct grammar and punctuation. Everything you do on LinkedIn, including the Answer section, helps to build your brand, so make sure your question is professionally written and visually appealing.

I would not click on the box that asks if you want to share the question only with your connections; if you do, it will be seen only by your first-level connections and not your whole network. It will limit both the number of answers you get and the exposure of your profile to the entire network.

Next, pick a category for your question; you can select one or two categories. Some areas even have a list of subcategories to select. Then you will see some prompts added by the clever folks at LinkedIn to try to dissuade you from asking certain questions. They want to know if what you are asking is a promotion of some sort or related to job hunting. That's because it's against their rules to post jobs, look for a job, or ask for connections on Answers. I recommend you don't do it, since there are so many places on LinkedIn to accomplish those tasks. Besides, your question will most likely be reported to LinkedIn and deleted, and you'll have a black mark on your account. Do not click *Yes* to these prompts; ignore them and hit the blue *Ask Question* button.

When you do, LinkedIn will give you the option to send the question to any of your contacts. You can select first-level connections, and the question will show up in their inboxes. I have never had a need for this; I want the widest exposure for my questions, so I always hit *Skip* on that step.

Once you send off your question, experts who watch their category will see your question and send you replies, which come right to your LinkedIn inbox. Your question stays open for a week, and then you rate the answers. Try sending a nice thank-you note to whomever answers your question by clicking on the *Reply* hyperlink under his or her answer. You have the chance to network with that person, and you never know where it might lead you; he or she might become a potential partner, client, friend, or center of influence. Offer thanks and an invitation to connect so you build your network.

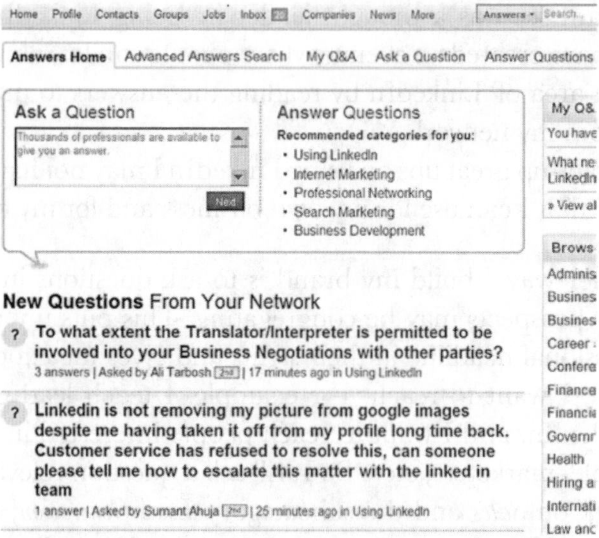

Figure 10-2. On the Answers Home page, you can begin the process of asking a question by entering the title or headline of the question, then clicking on the blue *Next* button to add details and select a category for your question. It's usually a good idea not to ask the whole question in the first box; instead, just put a summary and then add details in the second step.

Brand Yourself with Questions

The second reason I ask questions is free branding. When I'm not in need of technical advice, I ask a question in my topic of expertise, Using LinkedIn. Part of being a thought leader is not only putting content out there, but also starting conversations. As you know, social media marketing is built on a foundation of joining conversations. As the starter of conversations, you are building your brand in the areas where you want to be known.

So every few days I ask a question in Using LinkedIn, and it really helps me in many ways:

- I get more people clicking on my name, looking at my profile, and inviting me to connect—helping me grow my network.

- I am seen as a thought leader in Using LinkedIn because I have created an avenue where people can learn more about an area of LinkedIn by reading the answers to my question from my network.
- I pick up great tips on using LinkedIn I may not have thought of that I can use for my own business and for my clients.

Another way I build my brand is to ask questions in the fields where my prospects may be congregating. This puts my name and my professional headline in their sights and gives me exposure with the people I want to reach. For example, I teach lead generation using LinkedIn, and I want to reach people interested in that topic (salespeople, marketers, etc.). So I will ask a question relevant to that topic, click on *Sales* and the subcategory *Lead Generation*, and place my question where my prospects can see it and get to know me.

Make it part of your day to ask some questions in your field and in the field of your prospects, and you will develop your thought leader status and gain exposure to people who can buy from you.

Your Answer Command Center

By now, if you've followed my advice, you are asking and answering questions. So, how do you keep track of all your activity in this feature? LinkedIn provides you with a command center: From the top menu bar, click on *More* > *Answers* > *My Q&A*. There you can click on *My questions* and read answers to questions you asked in the past. You can click on *My answers* and see all the answers you have given and how many were rated "best."

Sometimes when you post a question and people respond, you might discover that the answers you are getting are not what you were looking for. Perhaps there was additional information you left out of the question or you need to word it differently. Also, people may be asking for more information. In the *My Q&A* section, you can click on *My questions* and add to your question.

Just locate the question you want to elaborate on, click on it, and then look for the *Clarify my question* link to open up a new text box titled Add Clarification. Add your new thoughts and click on the blue *Clarify question* button and your updated question will be available to everyone.

Extending Your Question Longer

When you ask a question, it stays open for only seven days. Let's say you have sparked a lively debate and you are getting lots of great responses. If you want to keep getting more answers, you can extend the life of the question. Or if you feel you have not gotten what you are looking for, that's another reason to want to get more answers.

In the *My Q&A* section, click on the question you want to revive and click *Re-open this question to answers*, which will open it up again for seven more days. You can ask only 10 questions a month, so you will need "answer credits" in order to keep your question open.

Sharing Your Questions

If you've asked a question that generated some great content, or you've answered a question that demonstrates your thought leadership, you have the ability to share that question with your network. Go to *More > Answers > My Q& A* and click on the question you want to share. Go to the question's page, and you will see a *Share This* hyperlink below the question. Click on it, and you can message the question to 200 LinkedIn contacts, bookmark it on del.icio.us, or grab a hyperlink to put it anywhere you want on the web.

One place for sharing questions is in your status update. Recently I asked a question in the Using LinkedIn section that got a great deal of solid responses; it was, "What's your biggest success to date on LinkedIn?" The answers were really inspiring, so I thought it would make a great item to share with my network. I clicked on the *Share This* link, got the URL for the question, and added it as a status update so my network could read the inspiring answers.

Another place to share questions is in Groups. I ask a lot of questions about using LinkedIn, and sometimes I think my groups would benefit from the answers. I click on the *Share This* hyperlink, start a discussion in the applicable groups where I think people will benefit from the responses, and add the question.

* * *

The Answers section of LinkedIn is extremely powerful. Get involved and start answering and asking questions and help take your brand to new levels; make new connections; find customers, partners, and work; and establish yourself as a thought leader on LinkedIn.

We began the chapter with the idea that LinkedIn is many things. In addition to what I mentioned, it's a powerful events calendar where you can extend your brand and your reach from the online to the offline world, and pull people to your seminars, meetups, and more. Let's learn how to do that in the next chapter.

Chapter 11: Promoting Yourself and Your Company with Events

Before the arrival of social media, if you wanted to advertise an event you were putting on, you had to spend cold, hard cash, place an ad in the local paper, and hope someone saw it. Or you had to take a chance by putting it in the classifieds in the "Event" section, where certainly no one was going to see it. Or you had to spend lots of money printing expensive brochures and paying for postage, which is something I am very familiar with, as that was my primary advertising medium when I ran a sales training company.

While you can still do all that, with social media you can get around much of that expenditure and wasted effort. With the LinkedIn Events feature, available free to everyone, you can target your audience for offline meetings and networking events and online webinars and teleseminars. You also have the possibility of others sharing your event so that it goes viral and is seen by many people throughout LinkedIn.

Creating an Event

To begin, go to *More > Events* from your top toolbar and click on *Events*. Once you do, you will find yourself on the Events home page (see Figure 11-1). Here you will see events you may be interested in based on your profile, events you have already created, and on the right the yellow *Create an Event* button. Click on it and you will be taken to the form for step one for creating your event.

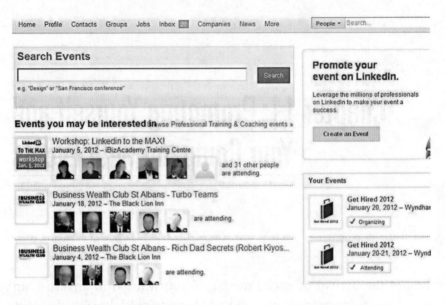

Figure 11-1. On the Events home page, you can begin the process of creating an event and publicizing it to your LinkedIn network. Click on the yellow *Create an Event* button to start the three-step process.

Step one is to fill out the following information:

- Name—your event title
- Date and time
- Venue name and address (or click *Virtual Event* if it's a teleseminar or webinar)
- Logo—where you upload your event logo.

After you fill in this information, click on the blue *Create Event* button and you are taken to step two.

In step two, you are able to do the following:

- Fill in the description of your event
- Select an industry category from a drop-down menu
- Add labels; these are keywords that describe your event and that people will be searching on
- Add a website address where people can go for more information

Complete this step, and you are taken to step three. Here you will find a Share Your Event box. There are buttons there which you click to send a tweet on Twitter to everyone following you, and also a Facebook button that takes you to your Facebook wall, where you can post the event. Also on this page you'll see a message from LinkedIn that says that your event has automatically been shared with your connections. That means that it appears as a status update on your profile, and on the home pages of all your first-level connections. When you are done with step three, click the blue *Finish* button to take you to your new LinkedIn Event page.

Publicizing Your Event

From your Events page, you will have the ability to share the event with others. (See Figure 11-2.) On the right you will see a box titled *Share This Event.* You will see three social media icons and a URL. The first icon is LinkedIn. Click on it, and you will see displayed the familiar LinkedIn *Share* box. In this box, you can share the event on any group's discussion board where you are a member, and you can also send it to individuals on LinkedIn.

The other two icons are for Twitter and Facebook, giving you another opportunity to publicize it to your fans and followers on those sites.

Finally, you'll see a URL that you can copy and paste to many places, including other social networks, your blog, your website, your email signature, and so on.

One of the reasons why you want to use the LinkedIn Event link is that you really want to get people to RSVP to your LinkedIn event in addition to going to your website. Any time people RSVP or express interest in a LinkedIn event, it shows up in their status and the news feed on the home page of every one of their first-level connections. So basically they are promoting the event for you, and thousands of people will see it and potentially click on it to read more about the event.

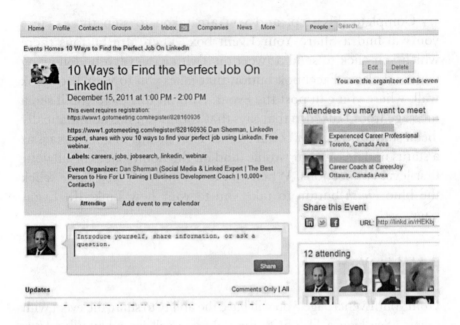

Figure 11-2. On your Events page, you will see details of your event, names of attendees, social media icons to help you spread the word, and a URL that you can use on the web to publicize the event.

Advanced Strategies for Events

Here are some other tips for getting the most out of the Events feature:

- When you register for a LinkedIn event, you can see all the attendees. Check it regularly and note the people you might want to meet by viewing their profiles. Send them a message up front introducing yourself and inviting them to connect with you on LinkedIn, since you have similar interests. This way you can grow your network and set the stage for meeting a potential client or partner. Also ask to meet with them at the event, where you can find out more about them.

- Use the attendee list for your event as a prospect list. Say you give a free training or you're organizing a meetup in your area of expertise. That attendee list is now a prospect list you can market to promote a paid service.

- Use the Search feature in Events to locate events coming to your area that will help you succeed, either by networking with people or attending a training. On the Events Home page, you will see a text box that says *Search Events* where you can type in keywords, such as an event topic or location. This is especially valuable when you are traveling and want to know about potential meetings in your areas of interest in the cities you are going to be visiting.

- On this page, you will also see events recommended to you by LinkedIn based on your profile, and a link to click on to browse events in your industry (again, based on your profile). Click on that link and you will be taken to a page showing events by location and industry that you can search through.

- If you provide services to groups that hold meetings—for example, you're a speaker, an audiovisual provider, or a caterer—you can search for local events. Go to *More > Events;* on the Events home page, type in your city in the search box. This way you can identify groups coming to your town and contact them and offer your services for the upcoming meeting, or the next time they visit your area.

* * *

No matter what kind of event you are hosting, be it a breakfast briefing, a networking night at a club, a webinar or seminar, or whatever, make sure to use Events to create buzz for your company and build a prospect list you can market to over and over.

Did you know that in addition to your personal profile, you can also have a profile for your company? And that if you have multiple companies, you can have a profile for each one? Read on and learn about the Company feature on LinkedIn, which gives you the chance to gather more prospects and customers for your business.

Chapter 12: Good Company: Adding Your Company and Following Others

When you register for LinkedIn, you do it as an individual, and most of your activities will be in branding You, Inc. as the leading expert in your field. That's because whether you work for yourself or for a company, you need to build your network and establish yourself as a thought leader every day. This will bring you business if you work for yourself, and it also prepares you to receive new opportunities if your job goes the way of the pay-phone booth manufacturers. (Just where does Clark Kent change into Superman these days?)

But that doesn't mean there isn't a place for company profiles on LinkedIn, because there is, and it's a very important area to get to know. In the Companies section, you can promote your own company or the company you work for and provide an entertaining, multimedia display of information. You can also use the Companies area as one of the most powerful prospecting and information tools you will ever use to seek out new business, find new opportunities, stay up to speed on your industry, and, if you're job hunting, locate the perfect position.

Listing Your Company

Let's talk first about the benefits of creating a Companies page for your enterprise. To get your company profile started, go to the Companies page by clicking on *Companies* on the top toolbar. This will take you to the Companies Home page (see Figure 12-1) where you can begin the process by clicking on the *Add a Company* link on the far right. You'll be taken to a page where you enter your company name and company email address. Note that you cannot use an email service address like Gmail or Hotmail; it has to be a company address, such as Hulk@TheClobberingCompany.com.

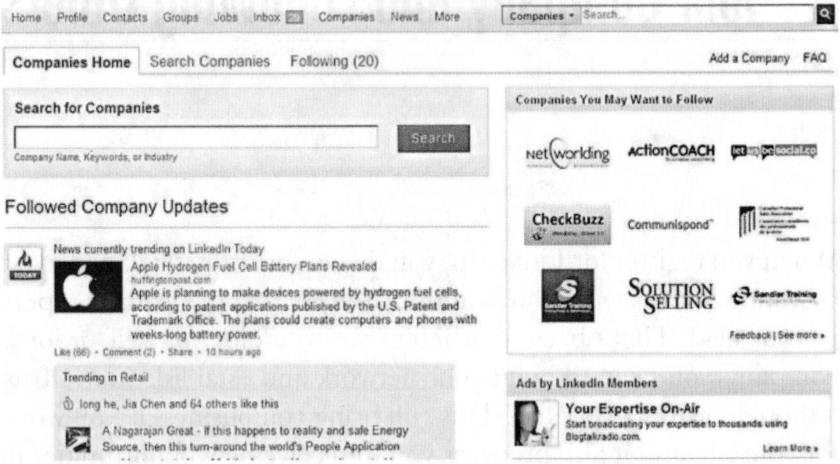

Figure 12-1. On the Companies Home page, you will see a text box for searching for company pages, and over on the far right a blue hyperlink that says *Add a Company*, which will take you to the Add a Company form.

What if you haven't registered with LinkedIn using your company email address? It's simple enough to add. Remember, you can associate as many email addresses as you like with your personal LinkedIn account. To add your company email address to your profile, simply click on *Settings* under your name in the upper corner of the screen; click on the *Change* hyperlink next to "Primary Email" in the upper left. This will bring up the *Add & change email addresses* box, where you can add your company email address, then click the blue *Close* button.

Now, back to setting up your company page. Once you have finished adding your company to the site, you will get a message from LinkedIn to check your company email inbox to confirm your identity. Then once you click on the link LinkedIn sends you, you're approved, and you can start to fill in your company profile. Here are some of things you will want to add:

- **Company Type.** Here you will put if it's a public company, a partnership, privately held, and so on.
- **Company Size.** Select from myself only to 10,001+.
- **Company Website URL.** Add your website here, and don't forget the http://.
- **Main Company Industry.** Select your industry from the drop-down menu.
- **Company Operating Status.** List your company's status.
- **Year Founded.** List the date your company began operations.
- **Company Locations.** Here you can list five different locations.
- **Image.** Add a picture that represents your company, using a PNG, JPEG, or GIF file up to 2MB.
- **Logo.** Add a standard logo (100 × 60 pixels) and a square logo (50 × 50 pixels) for use in network updates.
- **Company Description.** Tell the world what it is your company can do and how it can help them.
- **Company Specialties.** Here you can zero in on the products and services your firm offers.

When you've completed this page, click the blue *Publish* button in the upper right. Don't refresh the page or leave the page before clicking *Publish* or you will lose all your hard work!

Adding Details About Your Company

When you look at your company's page, you will see four tabs across the top: *Home, Careers, Products,* and *Insights.* (See Figure 12-2.) The *Home* page will show you all the information you added, a text box for adding a company status update, a list of your recent company

141

updates, and two buttons: *Follow* and *Admin tools*. When people land on your page and click *Follow,* they are able to keep up to date with changes that are happening at your company. When you click on *Admin tools,* LinkedIn provides a drop-down menu with options to edit the page, add a product or service, view analytics about your page followers and page views, or delete the page.

Figure 12-2. The company page you create will have four tabs across the top. There is also a text box for creating a company status update, a button that allows others to follow your company, and a button leading to your page administration tools.

The *Careers* tab offers you the opportunity to post a paid job ad for your company on LinkedIn. That's an option, but remember, every group has a free job board that is titled *Job Discussions* under the group's *Jobs* tab if you want to save money.

On the *Products* tab, you can add your company's products by clicking on the *Admin tools* button and choosing *Add product or service*. On this page, you choose whether it's a product or a service, and then you can add the following:

- The category of product or service
- The product or service name

- An image
- A description
- A list of key features
- A disclaimer
- The website for the product or service
- Company employees on LinkedIn who can answer product questions
- A special promotion
- A YouTube video

This section is a great way to drive traffic to your site or sites. You will want to add the URLs where you want people to go when they click images. You can add up to three images (640 × 220 pixels) and URLs, and LinkedIn will create a rotating spotlight module (or carousel) to display on your company page.

Also on this page, you will see a link that says *Request Recommendations*. Just as you should seek out as many personal recommendations as you can, you should also ask for recommendations for your company page. When you click on the link, you will get a text box you can use to ask for recommendations from your LinkedIn contacts. The more social proof you have for your company, the better, and these recommendations will be seen by anyone considering purchasing products and services from your company.

With the recommendation box, as always, LinkedIn gives you a prewritten subject line and request, but I suggest that you customize everything you do on this site. So erase what LinkedIn gives you and write something personal to the people you are approaching. Remember, you are asking them to take time out from their busy day to help you; the least you can do is personalize your request.

Finally, on the *Insights* tab, you will find a display of your employees who have new titles, employees who have left your firm (i.e., gone on to greener pastures), what companies your employees came from, and company pages that people who viewed your page also visited. Near each company listed is a *Follow* hyperlink allowing you to follow those pages and do a little "research" on firms you may be competing with.

Create a page for your company, and you will have one more corner of the web in which to promote your business and educate your prospective clients. Just like a website, it can be a multimedia extravaganza, but it's better than a website, because you can add social proof in the form of recommendations from your connections, and readers can click through and see who is recommending you. Anyone can make up quotes for a website (not *you*, of course). Company page recommendations are from real people whose profiles can be accessed, which makes them very powerful.

Creating a Company Status Update

According to LinkedIn, there are over two million company pages, and half of all members are following companies. So how can you create engagement with customers, prospects, and potential employees? LinkedIn has added status updates for companies for this purpose so that company pages are more like Facebook business pages.

Company Status Updates are posts you can make to share anything from company news to product releases to promotions to relevant industry articles. Company posts can be seen on your company's *Home* tab by any LinkedIn member. People who follow your company will see the posts directly on their home pages.

All LinkedIn members have the ability to view posts, click on embedded links, or view videos. They can also comment, like, or share a post. Company Status Updates will enable you or anyone you have assigned as administrator of your company page to post updates up to 500 characters in length to the *Home* tab of the page.

To create a Company Status Update, the first thing you need to do is correctly affiliate yourself with the company. In order to do that, you must update your LinkedIn Personal profile to reflect that you are currently working at the company after you created a company page on LinkedIn.

The way you do that is to click on *Profile > Edit Profile*, go to your Experience section, and click on *Edit* next to the position that correlates to the company page you just created. On the Edit Position page, click on *Change Company* next to your company's name. Then erase the company name and begin retyping it. LinkedIn will display all the companies that have pages as you type, so select your company from the options LinkedIn provides. Click on the *Update* button to save your changes. In doing so, your profile will be synched to your company page.

When you are correctly affiliated, you will see a little note card icon that looks like a sticky note next to your company name on your LinkedIn Profile in the Experience section. When you hover your mouse over it, your company information will appear in a dialogue box.

Once you start creating status updates, you will be able to see impressions and engagement on each update on your company page. (An impression is the number of views, and engagement counts likes, clicks, and shares.) Of course, the more followers your company has, the better, since the more exposure you will get.

So, make sure to work on getting followers by publicizing the page regularly in your LinkedIn profile status updates, in your email newsletters, in your email signature, and in any other client communications. Cross-promote your page by linking it to your LinkedIn Groups, Facebook page, Twitter feed, and your company website.

One of the strategies you can follow is to turn your LinkedIn company page into a traffic-generating machine the way that HubSpot has done. The Internet marketing company has loaded its *Products* tab with free Internet marketing ebooks and webinars in addition to a free 30-day trial of its inbound marketing software. When you click on a ebook or webinar-on-demand that you would like, you are taken to HubSpot's web page, where you first have to hand over information about yourself which helps fill its sales pipeline. (It asks for such things as your name, contact information, website, company size, and biggest marketing challenge.) Go to the HubSpot company page and see how it is driving traffic and collecting prospective client names from its outpost on LinkedIn.

Make Your Company Page Exciting

Once you start promoting your company page, you are going to want to make it an inviting place for your customers, prospects, potential partners, and employees to visit. That means continually updating it with great information. Here are some ideas to get you going:

- **Build out your tabs.** Fully develop your *Home*, *Careers*, and *Products* tabs, and optimize each one with keywords. This will improve your page's ranking in Google and LinkedIn search results, which will increase the reach of your company profile.
- **Promote your products.** On the *Products* tab, add descriptions and videos for each of your products. The "poster child" for creating a rich user experience on its company page is Hewlett-Packard (HP), the giant technology company. HP has over 800,000 followers on its page, and if you look at its Products tab, you will see how visually inviting it is. Visit HP's company page to see all that it is possible to do to leverage this free advertising medium.
- **Get social on your company page.** Allow users to make recommendations on your *Products* tab in order to provide social proof and make it interesting to read. Again, look at all the products HP listed along with the recommendations.
- **Add video testimonials.** For every product you add, you can add a link to a YouTube video. On the *Products* tab, click on *Admin tools* > *Add a product or service*. This is a great place to add clients talking about why they recommend the product.

Take time to create a LinkedIn company page and turn it into another form of communication with your prospects and clients. Use it as a traffic-generating machine, and expand the reach and presence of your company. It's an amazing free resource that you could be using right now to augment all your other marketing efforts.

Prospecting for Business Using Companies

Let's turn from promoting your own company to using this feature to rapidly fill your sales pipeline with qualified buyers. Basically, if you sell to companies, then the Companies section is your new best friend. If you have ever made a cold call, you know that "cold" is an appropriate designation. Often the reception you get on the other end of a cold call is "frosty," and I don't mean the famous jolly snowman.

What if you had an introduction to the person you want to meet? What if you could get to know people in the department you want to sell into who could turn you on to the person you really need to talk to? Enter LinkedIn Companies.

Select *Companies* from the top toolbar, and you'll be on the Companies home page. Type the name of the company you are targeting in the Search for Companies box, and you will be directed to its company page. Let's say I search on Apple. I get taken to its company page and I see the company description, but what I'm really interested in is on the right-hand side, where I see that there are 29,160 Apple employees in my network.

That breaks down to six first-level connections, 2,085 second-level connections, 545 group members, and the rest third-level connections. So overall, I can reach out to any of the more than 29,000 employees in my network through InMail (which costs money unless you have a premium account); through direct message if they are first-level connections or members of groups I'm in; or through introductions if they are second- or third-level connections.

Contacting People at Your Target Company

The first thing I might do is see who are first-level contacts that I can reach for free. I would read their profiles and get to know them a little bit better. Then I could send them a direct message introducing myself and asking them if they could steer me to the right people I need to talk to at Apple (or whichever company I'm targeting).

The next thing I can do is look to see who are my second- and third-level connections. If I want to reach one of them without paying for an InMail, I can click on her profile and look on the right-hand side to *Groups you share with (Name)*. If she and I share a group, it will appear as a hyperlink, and I can click on it. Then when I arrive at the group, I can click on *Members* on the menu bar and search for that employee by typing her last name into the *Search Members* box on the left. When I see the person I want, I hover my mouse over her name, and on the right I will see a hyperlink saying *Send a message.*

I might begin the message by introducing myself, explaining that we share a group, and asking for some information about her, her department, or her company. Always ask for information first— never sell on the initial contact. You are fact-finding at this point, so work on building a relationship.

If the person you want to reach has a premium account and is a member of OpenLink, then you can message him or her for free. And you could also use the InMail system if you pay for it or have a premium account.

Using Introductions for Prospecting

What if you are trying to sell into a department and you have no first-level connections in that department? Then you move on to second-level connections. At Apple, I have 2,085 second-level connections. That's a lot, and you might come up with a smaller number for the company you are targeting. Either way, I can look through all my second-level connections and find either just the person I'm looking for or at least one who works in the right department.

Let's say I want to reach John Smith, a second-level connection. First, I'll see if we share a group so that I can direct message him. But let's say we don't share any groups; I need to use the introduction feature, and here's how:

Under John's name, it says 20 shared connections (or whatever the number is). This is how we are connected—our first-level connections in common, so I have a lot to choose from. I click on John's name and go to his profile. On the right I see *How You're Connected to John S.* with links to all our shared first-level connections. I scan the list and pick the person I'm familiar with. Then I go to the information box on John's profile and click on the drop-down arrow on the gray button that says *Send John an InMail.* I will see the *Get introduced* link, click on it to reveal the Introduction Request form, pick a connection, and begin the process outlined in Chapter 8.

This way, I'm getting a warm introduction to John Smith. It's not guaranteed that the introduction will go through. But if the first-level connection is someone you know and your request is sincere, chances are good that that person will forward your introduction.

So first-level connections, second levels, and group members can all be approached; it's just a question of creating a strategy of whom you want to meet. Third-level connections can also be approached, but it's harder to do, since the introduction has to go through two people. There are also InMails and OpenLink messages to use as part of the process of prospecting. Try everything, and remember to ask for information and establish a connection before promoting anything.

Leveraging Company Information

In addition to providing connections to a target company and finding the right person to talk to, the Companies section gives you valuable employee and product knowledge about a firm you may be targeting for your offering or as a potential employer. (See Figure 12-3.)

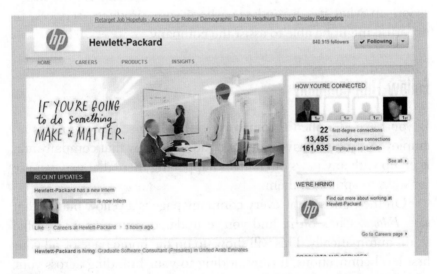

Figure 12-3. The company page offers a rich source of information for anyone prospecting or doing research on a potential employer.

Let's use HP as an example. First, when you are on its LinkedIn company page on the *Home* tab, you can view the *Recent Updates* section and see employee new-hire activity up to the minute. If you switch over to the *Insights* tab, you'll see senior-level employees who have been promoted within the organization.

How does this help you? Well, if you are selling into an organization or want to get a job there, you should know that whenever a new manager comes on board, she always takes a "new-broom" approach and brings in new suppliers and employees. If you see a new executive show up in terms of being hired or promoted who might be a target for your offer, or a potential new manager, click on her profile, see how you two are connected, and begin the process of getting to know her. Hopefully she will bring you into the company as a supplier or new employee.

Second, if you want to do any business with a company or get a job there, you had better be very up to speed on its products and services. No company today will appreciate an ill-informed sales representative or job candidate. In the case of HP's company page, you could click on the *Products* tab and get up to speed on 19 of its top products and watch videos on each one. So before you contact a company, visit its company page's *Products* tab and get the inside scoop on what it sells and see where your products, services, or expertise might be able to assist the company.

Follow That Company

If you have identified a company you wish to sell to or join as an employee, LinkedIn gives you an option to follow that company and keep up with any news or changes happening there that you can use for ways to approach them.

On the right side of every company page is a yellow button that says *Follow*. Click on it, and you've updated your personal profile status automatically. This will show up on the home page of all your first-level connections, further adding to your branding across your network.

Once you do this, the button turns gray and indicates *Following*. Now anytime that company creates a status update, it will show up in the feed on your home page. This is a great way to stay up-to-date with happenings at your target company, including events it is sponsoring, new product launches, job opportunities, management changes, and so on.

Another option for looking at the status updates of companies you are following is to click on *Companies* on the top toolbar, which will take you to the Companies Home page. On this page you will see Followed Company Updates, which displays updates from the companies you are following as they come in live. You are allowed to follow up to 100 companies, so if you are following a lot, like I do, you will see quite a mix of updates here—everything from a video tour of company offices, to a free ebook download, to a company's open positions around the country.

Also on the Companies page, you will see a tab on the right that says *Following*. Click on this to bring up the complete list of companies you are following. This very handy page keeps all the companies you are following in one neat place for you, so you can scan them all at once and add or delete ones according to your needs. From this list, you can click on an individual company you are following and go right to its page to read all its updates. In addition, LinkedIn provides a suggestion tool on the right side called *Companies You May Want To Follow*, which offers companies for you to follow that are similar to your current selections.

Use Company Pages to Create Opportunities

Thus, you can see that the Companies section is a data-rich area where you can create tremendous opportunities. There is an unlimited number of ways to use this area to enrich your professional goals. For example, you can do the following:

- Find, get to know, and target company employees you wish to connect with.
- Follow companies you want to sell to.

- Follow companies you may be thinking of acquiring, merging with, or partnering with.
- Identify windows of opportunity by reading the latest news about a company.
- Find ways to approach a company when new people come on board or are promoted.
- Use the section as a job-hunting tool by following potential employers in your area—or where you want to relocate to.
- Research competitors in your industry and get a leg up by seeing everything that is going on there.
- Follow previous employers to keep up-to-date on your colleagues.
- Stay current in your field by following the leading companies in your industry.
- Follow vendors that supply you with products, and learn what is new and exciting you may wish to get involved with.
- Follow your customers to make sure you know what they are up to, as a signal to see how else you can penetrate their business with more offerings, or an early warning sign if anything indicates they are searching for a new supplier.
- Look for updates where you can reach out to your connections at companies and use them as talking points and relationship builders.
- Follow companies that are influencing current events so you stay ahead of the curve.
- Follow start-ups and learn from their successes and failures.

* * *

It's a great idea to create a robust company page, update it often, and use it as a powerful way to connect with your customers and prospects. If you market to companies, then follow companies you want to sell to and use their company pages to gain insights and connections that would not be possible any other way. The information and contacts you discover will put you light-years ahead of your competition. Now let's look at one of the most powerful uses of LinkedIn that many on the "outside" (not a LinkedIn insider like you!) still believe is the only function of the site, namely, finding the perfect career. You will find that LinkedIn is the indispensible tool for landing your next job.

Chapter 13: Off to Work We Go: Finding Your Perfect Job

When it comes to the job-hunting game, I've sat on both sides of the table as a job seeker and as a hiring manager in corporate America. So I know that job hunting is never going to be fun or glamorous, or something we would undertake if we had a better option like winning the lottery or discovering we are related to Zuckerberg or Gates.

Still, it's a part of life that will always be with us and that we must master. Navigating the twists and turns, the ups and downs, the straightaways and the dead ends—that's what it's all about. Riding a roller coaster is about the best metaphor I can conjure up for job hunting—it's scary and exciting, and you are relieved at the end.

If you are currently looking for work, or you if you are working and want to keep your finger on the pulse of the job market to see what else is out there, you simply must be using LinkedIn. I have heard consistently from my recruiter friends that LinkedIn is now the number one place they go to first to fill a position.

LinkedIn is counting on that recruiter business and has created many resources for headhunters to ensure that it is doing everything it can to be the number one job source. It offers special recruiter membership levels and the ability to place paid job listings. They sell a service called LinkedIn Recruiter where recruiters can find, track, and stay in touch with potential hires and candidates. Recruiters are key to the LinkedIn business model; in its SEC filings to go public in

2011, LinkedIn stated that its recruitment product and service business represented 42 percent of its revenue (advertising made up 33 percent while paid memberships were 25 percent).

Whether recruiters use the services LinkedIn markets to them, post paid listings, or just hang out in Groups to meet candidates, it's the place they go first. Logically, it makes sense for recruiters and hiring managers to turn to LinkedIn first to check out the profiles and search through Groups and Answers for experts. With over 175 million profiles to select from, LinkedIn can be used by recruiters to attract the job hunters searching for a position as well as attract coveted satisfied employees away from other companies to a new opportunity.

So, yes, recruiters are as thick in LinkedIn as flies on honey. Not only are they there looking for you, but you can also reach out to them. You can be proactive and search for recruiters using the Advanced People Search (select *People* from the drop-down menu in the upper right, and click on *Advanced* by the magnifying glass): type the keyword *Recruiter* into the search box, find ones specializing in your region or in your field, and approach them about potential opportunities.

Reaching out to recruiters is certainly one way to use LinkedIn. But before you do that, the first step is to ensure that your profile is 100 percent complete and optimized using the tips in earlier chapters. Next, make sure you've invited all your previous managers to be first-level connections. That way you can request recommendations for your profile and also seek them out easily for leads and help with your job search. That includes past colleagues as well; make sure you invite as many of them as you can to be first-level connections so you have a solid network to call upon for help and posting recommendations to your profile.

Why LinkedIn Crushes Job Boards

If you are like most job hunters—and I know what that's like from personal experience when I was job hunting—you spend hours a day searching the job boards. And while job boards should be part of your strategy, there are so many reasons to shift your focus to making LinkedIn your primary job search site. Here's just a few of reasons why LinkedIn is superior:

- **Brand building.** On LinkedIn you can build your brand as the go-to person in your field by constantly updating and adding documents and presentations to your profile, getting recommendations, and participating in Groups and Answers.
- **Update your status.** You can let your entire network know that you are job hunting simply by updating your status on your home page. With one post, you can let your network of millions of people know you are looking by talking about a job fair you went to or a great informational interview you just had.
- **Networking.** Statistically, 60 percent of job hunters find their job through networking. LinkedIn lets you find a job by networking, but it takes it to a much more in-depth level. Through the people search and in the Groups and Companies features, you can find and connect with those who can help you find a job. Like they say, "It's not what you know, but who you know." Use all your connections—first level, second level, and third level—and fellow group members to reach the person who is hiring.
- **Credibility.** More than just a résumé posted on a job board, your LinkedIn profile lives side-by-side with all the activities that support who you say you are—for example, your participation in discussions throughout LinkedIn.
- **Find ability.** When you apply for a job, chances are good that the recruiter will use a search engine to research you just as you would a potential employer. Search engines favor information from social media and LinkedIn in particular, so if you have an optimized profile, it will be found on the first page of the search engine when your name is searched for, giving you an advantage over non-LinkedIn users.
- **Socializing.** Looking for a job can be lonely, especially if you just pore over job boards every day. LinkedIn is a living, breathing community of business professionals where you can

make connections for career advancement, read business advice from your peers, and share your insights with others. This makes LinkedIn a community of like-minded people— a place where "job hunting" is not a boring solitary task.

- **Immediacy.** With a job board, you submit your résumé and wait. And wait. And wait. On LinkedIn, you can find a worthwhile connection—someone in your target company or someone who might refer you to a hiring manager—and message him or her and often get a response right back.

- **Foot in the door.** With LinkedIn, you can request and arrange informational interviews by contacting people in your network who work at your target company. If the meetings go well, these people are likely to keep you in mind when a job opens or steer you toward an opportunity they know about. Remember that most positions are never posted anywhere; they are filled by referrals. So the more people you can meet and interact with, the better position you will be in when a job comes up matching your talents. That's why it makes sense to reach out to hiring managers at your target companies on LinkedIn whether they have an opening or not, and try to set up a call or short meeting.

- **Global:** Many job boards focus on an industry or a region; LinkedIn is worldwide.

The reason why LinkedIn is superior to job boards was explained by personal branding expert Dan Schawbel in an essay he contributed to *Dancing with Digital Natives* by Michelle Manafy and Heidi Gautschi (CyberAge Books, 2011), a book about the generation that grew up using the Internet:

The web has broken down hierarchies and connected everyone in disperse networks, so that you can reach individual employees directly at companies you want to work for, without applying through job boards. . . . The best method for companies, candidates, and recruiters to connect remains networking, according to ExecuNet, which found that just

10 percent of open executive-level positions are publicly posted online *(ExecuNet's 2010 Executive Job Market Intelligence Report, April 2010).* That number will probably drop to zero in five years. If you are looking for a job at any level today, it's time to follow the digital native's lead and start using those social networking sites you thought you were too old to join.

Schawbel goes on to say that a recent survey by Jobvite, a recruitment software firm, indicates "HR people use social networks and other online sources to research candidates," and 76 percent use LinkedIn.

Get the Low-Hanging Fruit First

Job hunting on LinkedIn is a much more participatory activity than using job boards, as connecting, networking, and sharing are the keys to success. But that does not mean there aren't job listings like the boards you've come to know and love, because there are. Jobs are not far away as soon as you log into LinkedIn. In fact, when you go to *Home > LinkedIn Home,* you will see *Jobs You May be Interested in* along the right-hand side, which LinkedIn has displayed based on keywords in your profile. Click on the title of the job and you will be taken to a page with the following information (see Figure 13-1):

- The full job description
- The name of the person posting it with a link to his or her profile
- Names of your LinkedIn connections who work at that company
- Jobs that are similar that have been viewed by other LinkedIn members
- A yellow button saying either *Apply on Company Website* or *Apply Now*

When you click on the *Apply on Company Website* button, you are naturally taken to the company's site, where you can fill in your information. If the job has an *Apply Now* button, clicking on it brings up an online application to which you can add a cover letter and résumé. When you hit *Submit*, all your information, including your LinkedIn profile, is forwarded to the hiring manager in an instant. That's another reason why you need to get your profile to 100 percent completion—it will help you make a great first impression (and you never get a second chance to make a great first impression)!

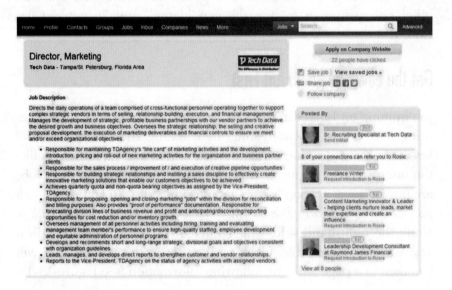

Figure 13-1. A company-paid job listing on LinkedIn provides you with the full description of the job, along with a hyperlink to the recruiter's profile and a list of all your connections who can introduce you to the person who posted the job.

Searching Paid Job Listings

After you look at the jobs LinkedIn has served you on a silver platter, you can then click on *Jobs* on the top menu bar and be taken to the Jobs Home page. That's where you can type in a keyword just like you would on other job boards and pull up jobs in your field of expertise and in the location you desire.

If you want to refine your search, click on the *Advanced Search* tab over on the right. There you can select criteria including industry, job title, company name, department type, location, and when the job was posted (see Figure 13-2). Premium members can also sort by salary ranges. Fill in your criteria, click on *Search*, and you will see your matches.

In that sense, LinkedIn can function like a job board. But the great thing is the feature I mentioned where you can see all the people in your network who can connect you to the person posting the job.

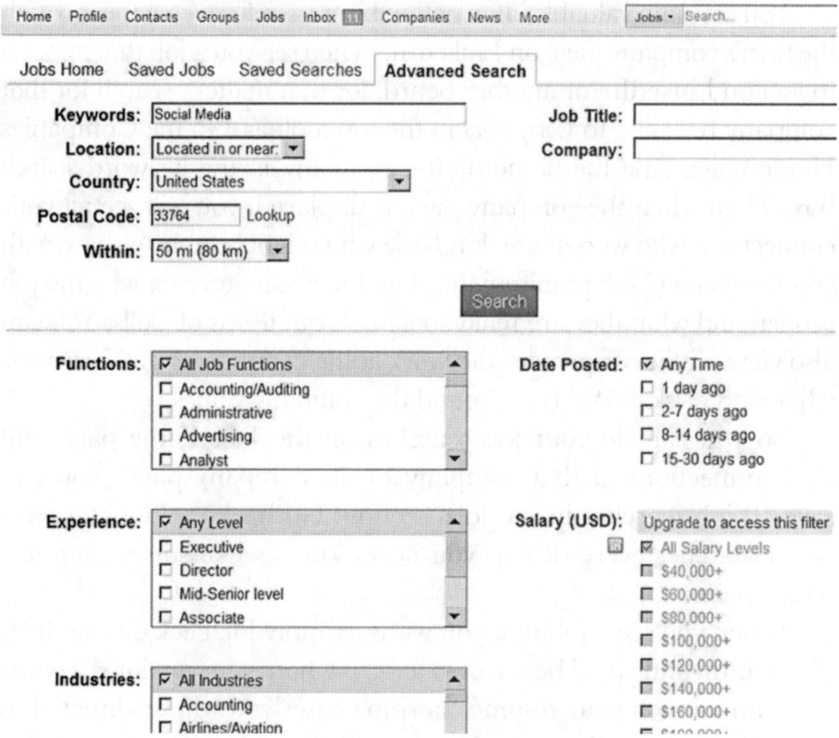

Figure 13-2. The Advanced Job Search functions like a job board, allowing you to search through all the paid job listings on the site.

For example, if I type *social media* in the keyword section and pick my location, which is Tampa, I get lots of jobs to choose from. So I pick out Sr. Marketing Manger at a local tech company and click on it. I see the job description and, in this case, 25 people in my network who know the person posting the job. So I can click through and see who might be able to make an introduction for me, thus turning a cold call or a random résumé into a warm call.

I can reach out to any of my connections and ask for an introduction. Also on the job listing page are the names of people in my network who work at the company. I can reach out to them, tell them I saw a job announced at their company, and try to get information on the job that I can use to better position myself to get the interview.

You can gain valuable information by cross-referencing the job with the firm's company page on LinkedIn. When see you a job that appeals to you on LinkedIn (or another board, for that matter), search for that company by going to *Companies* in the top toolbar. On the Companies Home page, type the name of the company in the keyword search box. Then when the company page is displayed, you will see all your connections who work there. Find one who might be able to share with you the "secret" job requirements. Get the inside story on why the job is open and what they are really looking for in terms of skills. You can also view profiles of people who work at the company to get a sense of what kind of skills and background the company values.

So you can do your job searches on the Jobs home page and find connections at that company on its company page. You can save 10 job searches in the Jobs section. Go back and look at your saved searches every day, as you never know when something new will appear.

When you see a job that you want to apply for, click on the *Apply Now* button and you'll be taken to a form where you can enter a cover letter and attach your résumé. In some cases you will be directed to the company's applicant tracking system. Just follow the instructions and apply.

Searching for Jobs in the Companies Section

The Companies pages will be a great boon to your job search. If you are targeting a certain company, a great strategy is to view its page.

Go to the top toolbar and click on *Companies* > *Search Companies* to get to the Companies Home page. Type your target company in the search box and visit that company's page. There you will get all the updates on the company—who's been hired, who's been promoted, and so on, as well as news about the company you can use to your advantage in interviews. You can see who in your network works at the company, and you can also see which college classmates of yours work there—valuable information for requesting an informational interview.

There are also job postings. If you click on the *Careers* tab on a company page, you will see all that company's paid job listings. Staying with Apple as my example, when I click on *Careers* on its company page, I see 45 job listings. If I click on any job headline, I will see a full job description and a button I can click to apply for a job. On the job description page, it also shows me my first-level connections at the company.

Here's a really creative way to find a job by leveraging the information on the company page. As I mentioned, each page tells you who's been hired recently. If you see someone who has taken a job you'd like at the company you're interested in, click on his name and visit his profile to see what company he recently left. What you have found is a company with a position to fill with someone who has the skills you possess. Maybe the company won't be replacing the person, but you never know until you approach someone at the company and let him know you are ready to step into the role of the departed employee.

Looking for Jobs in Groups

Another place to look for job postings is within LinkedIn Groups. Every group has a Jobs tab where every member can post a job, and I strongly urge you to take a look at that. Up until this point, you've been looking at paid listings. As a group manager, I know that not every organization wants to shell out the cash for a paid job listing, so it saves money by posting in Groups. In my Tampa Bay Marketing Professionals group, I get lots of these postings every day. So they are there...under the radar. That may be good for you as a job seeker, since fewer people see them than see the paid job listings.

Go to any group you've joined in a field you are interested in, click on the *Jobs* tab, and you will be on the group's Job page. Linked-In heavily promotes the paid job listings (it is a public company with pressure to make money), so it has downplayed the free posts, and you will initially only see the paid listings. But the free ones posted by group members are there to the left of the paid listings under *Job discussions*. Click on that hyperlink and you will see many open jobs. For example, in my Tampa group now, there are 11 posts, including one from a recruiter I know who has listed a multitude of jobs he has open. So don't overlook this feature; you might even make it a point to join groups in your field so you can get access to their job boards. Join 50 groups in your field and that gives you 50 job boards to explore.

The difference in finding a job in the Groups job area is that you don't have the lists of people in your network who work at that company displayed like you get when you click on a paid listing. But it's so easy to do research on LinkedIn with Companies pages and the Advanced People Search that it should not be a problem for you to find connections at any company.

Turn Your Profile into a Job-Hunting Machine

Let's go back to talking about your profile and go over some job-hunting strategies. Now, put yourself into the shoes of recruiters. They have deadlines and pressure, and the heat is on them to fill the stacks of job requisitions on their desks. They do the easiest thing first: they look for the cream of the crop. They do a people search and type in the keyword of the skill they need: *HTML coding*, or *Adobe Photoshop*, or *Chemical engineer*. The profiles that come up on top are most likely going to get looked at first, and those people will be called first.

That's why it's so important to have a position-ready, optimized profile. First, make sure your profile is 100 percent complete; if it is, your chances of being found will go way up. Next, make sure you have optimized it with the job skill for which you want to be found. Be specific—two to three words at most, and make sure that the keywords are in the four crucial places I mentioned in Chapter 6 on optimizing your profile.

Here's a tip: be that recruiter again and search for someone to fill a job that you are looking for by going to the Advanced People Search (click on *People* in the top right-hand menu; then click on *Advanced* by the magnifying glass). On the next screen, type in your keyword phrase and location and see who comes up. There's your competition for that job. Now look closely at the profile and see where the high-lighted keywords appear. At this point, your task is clear: add those keywords in a higher quantity in the exact same places in your profile and guess who will come up number one in that search next time? Yes, you. Try it today and you will see instant results.

Advanced Profile Tips for Job Hunters

If you really want your profile to be a job-hunting machine, here are more ideas. Turn your headline into an ad for your job hunting. Go to *Profile > Edit Profile*, click on *Edit* by your name, and in the section that's labeled "Professional Headline" announce to the world that you are seeking opportunities.

Write: "Actively Seeking an Opportunity to Bring My Extensive Sales Leadership Experience to Increase Profits." Or: "Seeking a Role in Advertising Copywriting Where I Can Create Compelling Groundbreaking Ads" or "Pursuing an Engineering Opportunity to Write Code for the Next Big Internet Success Story." In your headline, say what you are looking for, but say it in a way that demonstrates how you will add value to any company that hires you. Let's face it: recruiters and hiring mangers *only* care about what you can do for them, so broadcast it in your headline.

What this does is every time you make a post anywhere on Linked-In—for example, in Groups or Answers—people see your name and headline. If you make a great impression on people and they need someone like you—or know someone who does—you may be on track for an interview or possibly a new position.

Next, handle the Current Position section in your profile with care. If you list your last job there, you will only confuse people as to whether you need a job or not. And it's slightly unethical to say you work somewhere you don't. Remember, everything on LinkedIn brands you. Instead, I recommend putting "consultant" in for your current job; you could elaborate and say, "Consulting and looking for a full-time position." Another idea is if you manage a LinkedIn Group, you might want to use that title, since it brands you as an expert, it shows you are staying busy, and readers will know it's not a full-time gig. If you have a leadership role in a volunteer organization, you can put that as your current job.

Continuing on, use the Summary section (go to *Profile > Edit Profile* and click on *Edit* next to *Summary*) to create an ad for yourself as a job hunter. Talk about what the perfect position would look like for you, why you want it, and what about your experience makes you the perfect person for it. Create an ad for yourself, always keeping in mind making it value-oriented to the reader (i.e., what's in it for them if they hire you). A clearly spelled out Summary section should allow the reader to know right away if you are perfect for the job.

I recommend creating your job-hunting summary in an outline. Write it in MS Word first and copy and paste it into LinkedIn; that way you can spell-check it and use the cool bullets they offer. Here are my suggested headlines for your Summary outline:

About Jane Jobhunter: In this section, give a three- to four-sentence overview about your skills and talents and what you can offer a company.

How I Can Add Value to Your Organization: Here is where you would put a bulleted list of the different ways you can help a company.

Highlights of My Experience: Here in a bulleted list is where you can add very specific, quantifiable results you have provided to other companies; use numbers where possible.

What I'm Looking For: Here is where you put what kind of organization you want to join and where it is located.

How You Can Reach Me: Under this heading, put every single contact method you can think of so that recruiters can easily get in touch with you.

These are just suggested headlines. Modify them for your particular job search.

The next step is to make sure you add all the skills you possess and want to showcase to your future manager. Go to *More* on the top toolbar and click on *Skills & Expertise*, type a skill into the search box, and then click *Add Skill* so it shows up on your profile. Add as many as you can find that represent your skillset, up to 50 skills. And remember, with the *Endorsement* feature, you can have your first-level connections endorse your skills. When a connection endorses your skill, his picture with a hyperlink to his profile appears near the skill he endorses. The more people you have endorsing a skill, the more smiling faces appear by that skill.

Next, make sure you have recommendations for each of your profile jobs. Social proof is key. Aggressively seek out recommendations from everyone you worked with in your past jobs. Recruiters will give more weight to managers you reported to and customers you satisfied. Recommendations from coworkers are most likely shrugged off by recruiters, since it's too easy for people to trade recommendations with friends.

Focus on Accomplishments

It goes without saying that you should complete all the sections in your profile because recruiters and hiring managers will check you out on LinkedIn. In the Experience section, where you list past jobs, focus on your accomplishments, not just your responsibilities. If you increased sales by 25 percent, say so; if you cut costs by 15 percent, say it. Be specific. Hiring managers want to know the results of what you did at work.

Don't forget that you can also put any part-time work, consulting assignments, and volunteer positions if it helps bolster your reputation and credibility for the type of job you are looking for. In very specific terms, add your accomplishments there.

Use Box.net to Provide Your Résumé

Say a recruiter is looking at two LinkedIn profiles, and he needs to fill a job in a hurry. He needs to see a résumé fast; if your résumé is already on your profile, you have the advantage. The recruiter does not need to take time to call or email you for your résumé.

You can have your résumé available to recruiters by turning it into a PDF file and using one of the free applications on Linked-In called Box.net. On the top menu, go to *More > Get More Applications* and download Box.net. Set up a free account with that app and add it to your profile. You will then be able to upload your résumé (after removing any confidential information) so any recruiter or hiring manager can have it instantly. You will need a PDF creator such as Adobe, or just go to a FedEx Office location and have someone put it on a removable USB thumb drive for you.

Go Multimedia and Stand Out

Make your profile even more of a job-hunting machine by taking advantage of all the free applications on LinkedIn. As I mentioned, use Box.net to post your résumé and examples of your work (white papers you wrote, etc.). Use SlideShare to upload your portfolio or a PowerPoint document that explains your unique experiences and qualifications.

You might want to consider doing a video résumé. Put on your best outfit and have a friend video you in a well-lit room with no clutter in the background. (Empty beer cans, thongs hanging from the rafters, and a "water pipe" won't make a favorable impression.) Make it as professional as you can by filming in an upscale setting such as a conference room or an office you can borrow from a friend. Talk about yourself and your experiences, and let the video convey who you are and what can you bring to any organization. It's more powerful than a résumé or a profile full of text and gives a dynamic, well-rounded view of your abilities.

To upload your video to your profile, go to the top toolbar, click on *More* > *Get More Applications*, and select the SlideShare PRO application, add it to your profile, and upload your video.

Be Available and Show It

If you're looking for work, be sure to click the box next to *Career opportunities* in your contact settings in the box at the bottom of your profile. Click the link *Change contact preferences* to edit that section. You do that because your contact preferences must be consistent with the rest of your "job-hunting machine" profile or recruiters will dismiss you.

Leverage Your Alma Mater

Take advantage of your alumni status by connecting with people who went to your school. They may be in a position to give you an informational interview at a target company or even refer you to a hiring manager. To find them:

- Search the Group Directory for your alumni group, join it, and network with graduates of your school. You might also send a message through LinkedIn to the group manager, introduce yourself, and describe why you have joined the group. That person might be able to provide valuable insights and advice.
- Do an Advanced People Search with your school name as a keyword and use different variations of the school name, including acronyms (e.g., search University of California Los Angeles and UCLA).
- Use the *Find Classmates* function in the *Contacts* > *Add Connections* section and expand your graduation range to find even more alumni.

When you find a fellow alumnus with whom you want to network, ask for information first, then a referral. This way you can get to know the person and form a relationship, which could be the basis for him or her helping you out.

Find a Job Fair

Often local organizations and companies will post their job fairs and open houses in LinkedIn Events. This is a great opportunity to meet hiring managers and recruiters face-to-face and practice your 30-second elevator pitch (so named because if you got into an elevator with someone you needed to sell yourself to, you'd have just a few seconds to impress her before she got out of the elevator).

On the top toolbar, go to *More > Events* and on the Events home page, type into the Search Events box words that will help you find the right event. Try writing in the name of your city or region and *jobs*, *open house*, or *career fair*.

When I type in *Tampa job fairs*, I get five events that are coming to my town in the immediate future where I can go and meet hiring managers. You also can do a search by profession. When I type in *social media job fairs*, I get four pages of social media job fairs around the country I could attend. You can also type in the name of a company and *job fair* or *open house*.

Experiment with different search terms until you find events where you can go—and get out from behind that computer! Even if you don't land a position, you can sow the seeds for the future by meeting recruiters and hiring managers at target companies.

Participate in Groups

Groups can be one of the most powerful tools in your job-hunting arsenal. You can join 50, so I encourage you to maximize this feature and join up to the limit. Consider joining groups that will contain professionals you'd like to work for and with—and get active! Don't sit on the sidelines. Respond to interesting posts with your own thoughtful input. Every time you do, it gives you one more chance to be noticed by people who can potentially help you. Additionally, recruiters often hang out in industry-specific groups looking for experts they can approach.

In Groups you want to be real and helpful. Connect with as many people as you possibly can who participate in the groups, as you never know who can help you find a job. As a group member, you are allowed to direct-message other members. So don't be shy, and reach out to someone who made an interesting post or who works someplace you would like to know more about.

In addition to joining groups in your field, consider joining some of the thousands of groups devoted to job hunting. Some of these groups are massive! For example, in the upper right-hand corner in the search box, select *Groups*, type in *jobs*, and the first group you will see is Jobs: Job Opening, Job Leads and Job Connections! with over 600,000 members. The next one, Jobs: Job & Career Network, has over 340,000 members.

These groups are filled with job seekers like yourself, but also hiring managers and recruiters who are posting jobs. You'll see that in addition to the many job posts, there will be helpful and free advice on résumés, interviewing, and job search strategies posted by career coaches. Join some of these Jobs groups and take advantage of the postings and advice to accelerate your search.

Answer Questions to Establish Your Brand

The one thing about job hunting is that there tends to be lots of downtime between interviews. Put that time to good use by answering questions in your field and becoming a thought leader on LinkedIn. You never know if someone in your field who has a job open or knows a job open will read your responses. I have heard from my friends in the recruiting business that headhunters often hang around in the Answers section looking for potential candidates.

Since your headline shows up next to your well-written, solidly expert answer with your job-hunting headline (e.g., "Actively Pursuing a Career to Increase Efficiency and Productivity as a Call Center Manager"), you may be contacted about a job. Make it a part of your job-hunting day along with checking openings to answer a set number of questions. By posing thought-provoking questions, you will also position yourself as a thought leader in your field and someone people admire and want to know. Remember, you can answer an unlimited number of questions and ask 10 questions a month. Asking questions gets your name out there and contributes to the brand you are building on LinkedIn.

Also when you take part in Answers, it shows up on your profile. Along the right side of your profile (go to *Profile* > *View Profile*) you will see (*Your name's*) *Q and A*. Any questions you have asked will appear there, and if you earned Expert status by having your answer rated the best, you will have a cool star and a description of the category in which you have expertise. This shows recruiters and hiring managers that you are actively taking part in conversations in your field and keeping up to date.

Search on Your Specialty

Say you have a specific specialty, such as a programming language like JavaScript, XHTML, or Ruby on Rails. You could use the Advanced People Search to find companies in your area that hire people like you.

Select *People* next to the search box in the upper right of the screen, and then click on the *Advanced* hyperlink by the magnifying glass to get to the Advanced People Search page. Type your specialty in the keyword box, and select your location. You will then be presented with lots of profiles of people who have your skill. Scan them and see what companies they work for. Then, find out how you can approach those companies to see if they have any openings. At least try to get an informational interview so you have someone you can keep in touch with and stay top of mind with when a spot does open up.

Upgrade to a Job Seeker Premium Account

LinkedIn offers so much with its free account to assist you in your job search it might just do the trick. But if you want to add to your capabilities, consider upgrading to a Job Seeker Premium account by going to *Jobs* > *Job Seeker Premium*.

When you get this account, LinkedIn puts a little briefcase icon near your name on your profile notifying recruiters that you are looking. You also get more benefits such as:

- Placement as a featured applicant when you apply for a job
- More job-searching features
- InMails to contact people outside your first-level connections
- A complete list of everyone who has read your profile

Look through the Job Seeker Premium account options and see if they appeal to you for the price.

Do Research for Your Interview

When you do get an interview, look for the organization to which you are applying in Companies in LinkedIn; read up on the company so you look well informed. Also check out the profile of the person who is going to interview you, print it out, and bring it with you. If you don't know who is interviewing you, call and ask the company up front who the interviewer is, and if it is a team interview, try to get everyone's name and look at all their profiles.

You can look for areas of common interest that will break the ice with the interviewer. By reading his profile as well as recommendations he wrote for others, you get to know his likes and dislikes so you are prepared to shine in the interview. You might see that he once worked at a company you knew well or admired. Or perhaps he does volunteer work for a cause you also support. By mentioning these things in the interview, it will impress him because you cared enough to research him and didn't just walk in cold. It also shows that you are social media savvy, which is important to every business on the planet today.

Social Media Job-Hunting Advice from a Career Coach

As we end this chapter, I thought it would be a great idea to call on a career coach for a few closing tips. Lee Silverstein specializes in helping his clients find work quickly by using social media to be discovered by recruiters and hiring managers. Lee has 29 years of experience in leadership and organizational development, training, interviewing, and hiring. Lee told me:

> Here are the top 10 social media job-hunting strategies I share with my clients.
>
> 1. Do not "cut & paste" your résumé into your LinkedIn profile! When you interact with hiring managers and/or recruiters, one of two things will happen: they will find you on LinkedIn and then ask for your résumé or they will get your résumé and then check out your LinkedIn profile. In either scenario do you really want them to say, "Yeah, I already know that"? LinkedIn provides you an opportunity to share additional information about yourself and to do so in a different "voice." Take advantage of it.
> 2. The past is the past; target everything else for the future. If your previous job was in accounting but you want to get into financial planning, then be sure your headline, summary, specialties, and skills (more on this one later) are all targeting financial planning.
> 3. Personalize your LinkedIn profile summary and write it in the first person. Writing in the first person shows you as "human." Your summary should include keywords focused on the position (not the job) you are interested in. It should also answer the following questions:
>   - What do you do?
>   - How do you do it?
>   - Who do you want to do it for?
> 4. Always remember, when searching for a new career, you are selling; the product is "you." Your goal is for the buyer (the hiring manager or recruiter) to want to buy what you're selling (you). Anthony Parinello, in his book *Selling to VITO (the Very Important Top Officer)*, states

that successful salespeople prove that their product can help a company in at least one of the following four areas:

- Increase revenues
- Improve efficiencies
- Reduce costs and/or expenses
- Be in legal/regulatory compliance

In your LinkedIn profile and résumé, you must cite specific examples where you have done at least one of these four things in each job you've held.

5. Treat your connections like your garden; grow and nurture them. Use the steps Dan mentions in Chapter 7 to build your connections. Nurture them by writing recommendations, joining and participating in their groups, and introducing them to others.

6. Take advantage of all that the Skills & Expertise section has to offer. This often-overlooked section of LinkedIn is like one-stop shopping for job seekers. Go to the top menu and click on *More > Skills & Expertise* and you will find yourself on the Skills & Expertise home page. Enter your skill or expertise and click on *Search*. For each skill that you enter, you will find:

- Connections (first, second, and third degree) that share the same skill
- Companies that specialize in that skill area
- Posted jobs looking for individuals with that skill
- Suggested groups you can join related to that skill

7. You get what you give. Be generous (yet sincere) with your LinkedIn recommendations, leave positive comments on blogs, and retweet other people's articles.

8. Build your professional online reputation. When you do an online search for "you," what do you find? If your answer is "nothing" or just your LinkedIn profile, you have work to do. Companies want to see that you have a reputation as an expert in your field. A quality LinkedIn profile is a great first step. You should also set up professional

profiles on Google (https://profiles.google.com/), and the free, personal profile sites About.me and Flavors.me.

9. Read blogs, especially those related to your field. Bloggers are a great source of information and make great connections. Leave positive comments where appropriate, and share the posts that you particularly like on LinkedIn, Google Plus, and Facebook, and via Twitter.

10. Spend time in the "virtual hangouts" of people you want to connect with. Interested in working at Dell, Inc.? Did you know that Michael Dell is very active on Google Plus?

11. I know Dan asked for 10 tips, but I always believe in giving a bit extra! Get to know your connections I.R.L. (In Real Life). You won't land your next career sitting in front of your computer all day. Pick up the phone and call your connections and find out more about them. If they're local, arrange to meet over coffee. Don't forget that post-meeting thank-you note.

For more information on Lee's company, visit http://tampa bayjobcoach.com.

Whether you are on the roller coaster of a job hunt or checking the waters to see what's out there, I am convinced that making LinkedIn a big part of your day will help to further your career. Since people hire people—and there are over 175 million of them on LinkedIn—you want to expand your opportunities by interacting with the other professionals on the site as much as you can. Let me end this section with these closing tips:

- Get the word out: make sure as many people in your network as possible know you are looking for work.
- Be active: add to the group discussions, answer questions, and share interesting articles you have found with your network. The more value you can provide, the better and more visible you will be on LinkedIn.
- Be proactive and meet with people by picking up the phone (yes, that electronic device in your pocket).

- Spend time researching your contacts at your target companies for potential hiring managers or future work colleagues, and then contact them directly.
- Build two-way relationships. LinkedIn is about helping others first, and that goodwill may come around to you.
- Expand your job-hunting research beyond LinkedIn to Google. Using Big Brother Google (just kidding, guys), you can actually set up automatic notifications of any topic written about on the web, and they will be sent right to your email inbox. It's called Google Alerts, and it's a free service. You can tell Google to notify you when your target company is mentioned anywhere on the web; the same goes for a hiring manager you are targeting, a certain position you are going after, or happenings in your field. Go to http://www.google.com/alerts to set up as many notifications as you like.

* * *

There are so many ways to track down career opportunities on LinkedIn it's hard to imagine the site coming up with a new one, but LinkedIn did. It's called Signal, and it allows you to isolate any of the conversations among the millions of people on the site that have to do with hiring in your field and location. Let's go on to the next chapter and see what Signal is all about and how it can help you find a job that probably has not even been posted.

Chapter 14: Laser Focus Your Searches Using LinkedIn Signal

Find a Job with Signal

LinkedIn has so much to offer, and like all social media, it's a living, breathing community with split-second updates. What if you could pick a keyword and see who was talking about it throughout your entire network and in all the groups you belong to? Well, LinkedIn took a page from Twitter and created Signal, which you access for free by going to the top toolbar and clicking on *News > Signal*. (See Figure 14-1.)

For several years we've been able to isolate thoughts in the overwhelming rush of ideas that is Twitter by going to www.twitter.com/search, typing in a keyword, and seeing in real time who was talking about any topic. You can type in your town, your industry, a person's name, a company, or whatever, and see who is talking about it on Twitter.

LinkedIn developed its own similar search engine that you can use to look through all the updates being made throughout your network in status updates, group posts, LinkedIn Answers, profile changes, and so on. All the searches can be isolated by different variables, including such things as location, groups, industry, and update type.

Figure 14-1. Signal provides up-to-the-minute intelligence for anyone marketing a product or service or searching for his or her next job.

It's basically a new type of intelligence tool for you to use to keep up with anything you are researching. The applications for job hunters are impressive. Let's say you are looking for a job in New York City. You would go to *News > Signal* and type in the keyword *Hiring*, select all your levels of connections, check *New York City* in location, and see up to the minute anyone referencing in posts or updates about hiring in the Big Apple.

Let's say I want to make my Signal job search–specific. So since we're talking about the Big Apple, what if I put *Apple* in the company section? When I do this, I get a page full of people who work for Apple who have posted an update talking about hiring people for Apple. You could also type in the name of a hiring manager or a recruiter and pull up all that person's updates to see if she is talking about hiring. You could put in the name of a target company and get updates on that company, which might include the opening of a new location that needs staffers.

All of these searches can be saved, too. Just click on the + *Save* button at the top, and your search will be saved so you can go back to it throughout the day. One thing I've noticed is that the settings are somewhat sensitive. If you do one search but then decide to do another, you can't just change the criteria. You need to go back to *News > Signal*, refresh the entire page, and then enter your new criteria; otherwise, it saves criteria from the last search.

With Signal, you might just find people posting that they are hiring and be the first to contact them, since it's a good chance they haven't taken out job ads or officially posted the jobs anywhere. So it's a good idea to keep an eye on Signal throughout the day and learn how to use it as an up-to-the-minute job board.

Build Your Business with Signal

If you are actively marketing products and services, you can use Signal as a form of intelligence gathering. Search on your company to find out what people are saying about you. Search on your products or the ones sold by your competitors. Do a search on your competitors to see how they are positioning themselves.

They say that timing is everything. If you are in sales, do a search on companies you are targeting and you will get real-time updates you can use as icebreakers to start conversations with people at that company. Look for changes in the company that indicate new pains or needs you can solve. Try adding the word *recommend* in your search next to your product category to see if you can find anyone asking for recommendations for what you have to sell.

Here are a few examples of how I'm using it: I do a search on social media thought leaders to catch up with what they are saying. I type their names into the keyword search box and then read all their updates. I also do a search on my profession, LinkedIn Training, to see what my competitors are up to and see what I can learn from their approaches and their successes. I study how they promote their courses, when they offer them, and how much they charge so I can stay competitive with the market.

*   *   *

As you can see, Signal is a multipurpose tool for looking for opportunities, creating competitive intelligence, and keeping up to date with your chosen field. Try Signal, and let it isolate the ideas and comments that will help you in your career. Now, let's turn to what is arguably the hottest trend this year, mobile computing, and see how LinkedIn fits into the picture and how it's possible to stay connected every minute to your valued connections.

Chapter 15: Going Mobile: The Power of LinkedIn on the Go

You *Can* Take It with You

You don't have to walk far anywhere in this country (or many others, for that matter) to see almost everyone strolling with their head down, eyes fixed on their mobile phone, with their thumbs twitching out messages or buying products. It seems like the mobile revolution has completely engulfed us, and some statistics I found on a blog by Site-wire, an online marketing agency, back that up:

- There are 285 million mobile subscribers in the United States, which is 91 percent of the population.
- Mobile devices are predicted to pass personal computers as the Internet access device of choice by 2013, according to Gartner Research.
- An estimated $2.2 billion in sales of physical goods were purchased by mobile phone in 2010.
- By 2015, more than 50 percent of mobile users will participate in mobile banking.
- Mobile retail is expected to reach $12 billion by 2014.
- Business-to-business mobile marketing is expected to grow from $26 million in 2009 to $106 million in 2014.

Those are just some of the stats that show we truly are becoming a mobile device–based world. For everything you can imagine doing on a PC, "there's an app for that" on your mobile device. Fortunately, LinkedIn is part of the mobile revolution and provides a free application, or app, which I heartily endorse.

I have to tell you that using applications came at a cost for me. I had to kick my old cell phone—which had become a virtual extension of my arm—to the curb, something I never thought I would do. (The name of the old phone starts with a *B*, and it just would not abide apps or graphics at all.) I bought a newfangled device running Google's Android operating system, a Samsung Galaxy Epic. Now I can take LinkedIn with me wherever I go. Whenever I have a few minutes downtime, such as while waiting in a slow post office line or grabbing a quick soup and salad at the local Panera's, I log onto the mobile app.

This app is cleverly designed to provide a great deal of the functionality of the site. On the LinkedIn mobile app, I can:

- Check my inbox and see if anything needs immediate attention
- Peruse updates from my network and make comments
- Review my groups and read posts and comment
- Check out profiles of people in my network whom I may wish to do business with
- Read news brought to me by LinkedIn
- Look through LinkedIn's suggestions for people to connect with

Sales professionals, business owners, job hunters, and nearly anyone marketing a product will find it invaluable, as you can research a contact you just made or look up someone you are about to give a presentation to or meet in an interview. I find it very handy, and if you have an iPhone or Android phone, you may enjoy it too. If you don't have a smartphone that handles apps, then perhaps it's time for an upgrade.

LinkedIn Is for Tablets Too

Is the computer dead? Will we all be computing soon on tablets only, the desktop and laptop computers of our youth just a distant memory?

The debate rages on, and all I can say is my tablet computer is just great. Now, I'm not ready to ditch my laptop just yet because typing fast on a tablet is a skill I have not yet mastered. But for important tasks like playing pinball, backgammon, and Angry Birds, and extending my workday into the evening hours as I sit on the couch watching TV and answering emails, it's a real joy.

My tablet is an iPad, an amazing device and my first Apple product. I was a diehard PC user my whole life until Apple opened up one of its insanely profitable Apple stores near my home with its insanely great products out on full display. After a few weeks of hanging out in the store and playing with an iPad, I just had to have one. No wonder those stores are so profitable! (According to an article in the tech blog Mashable, Apple stores make more money per square foot than any other U.S. retailer.)

I quickly became a client of the Apple app store, and downloaded the free LinkedIn iPad app. The app is also available for Android tablet owners through the Google play store. When you open up the app, you see three main boxes. Click on the first, labeled *All Updates*, and you are taken to a screen that you can page through left to right just like a popular news app called Flipboard. You'll see updates from your connections, news stories, posts from LinkedIn groups where you're a member, and so on.

Click on the second box, marked *You*, and you'll have access to your profile, people who have viewed your profile, your recent activity on the site, your connections, and so on.

Finally, you can click on the third box, titled *Messages*, which takes you to your LinkedIn inbox where you can read your mail and notifications and also take action on LinkedIn invitations to connect.

The LinkedIn tablet app is another great way to stay in touch with your network on the site and also have access to trending topics through the news stories and updates. It's just one more way that information to help your business and career is readily available at your fingertips.

* * *

Throughout the book you've learned about the many ways in which LinkedIn can help you create and nurture the relationships that will take your career or business to the next level. But it goes without saying that you don't just log in, set up a profile, and watch money fall from the heavens. You have to work it on a regular basis. It's not a "set and forget" proposition. After all, your cell phone is a spectacular device, but it doesn't make sales calls for you, right? If you are in business of any kind, LinkedIn is something that should become part of your daily routine—as much as grabbing a cup of joe at Starbucks or checking your email. In the next chapter, I will talk about what kinds of activities you should consider as making up your everyday routine on LinkedIn.

Chapter 16: The Daily Approach to Success on LinkedIn

As you know by now, I'm an advertising guy, and I love good ad slogans. This one from the Navy recruitment ads from years past best sums up this chapter: "It's not just a job. It's an adventure."

That's the way I look at LinkedIn. Every day I log on and I'm not sure whom I am going to meet, who's going to contact me with an opportunity, or who is going to teach me something I need to learn or lead me to a new resource that helps boost my business. It's an adventure because I constantly meet people from around the world while sitting at my computer, and many of these people I will learn from and end up either partnering with or providing solutions to help their businesses.

But just as any adventure requires a little effort, so does LinkedIn. You get out of it what you put into the site. So it's a good idea to create a ritual of what you're going to do on LinkedIn every day, and the first place to start is with your status update.

Making the Most of Status Updates

When you wipe the sleep from your eyes and log into LinkedIn in the morning, it's a great idea to update your status box. Go to *Home > LinkedIn Home* and you will see your picture next to an empty text box that says *Share an update*. (See Figure 16-1.) Every time you create an update and click the *Share* button, your update appears on the home page of all your first-level connections.

You will see a paperclip icon and *Attach a link* under the status box. You click on that and an *Add URL* message comes up with a box to add a website address. That way you can attach a website you want people to visit, a link to a press release announcing a new product or upcoming event, or an interesting article or blog post you want to share with people. By adding valuable content to your network feed every day, you help brand yourself in your field as someone who is knowledgeable and helpful. You can also promote a webinar or teleseminar and attach a URL that takes people right to the signup page.

Also, you will see the blue Twitter bird logo and checkbox on the right-hand side by the *Share* button. When you select that by clicking on it, your Twitter feed will also be updated. So in my case, with one update I alert 27,000 people—my 16,000 LinkedIn connections and 11,000 Twitter followers.

Figure 16-1. The status update allows you to share interesting content with your network and engage and remain top of mind with thousands of people on a daily basis.

The update is a great way to share interesting content or promote anything you are working on and remain top of mind with your network. With your status update, you can:

- Promote networking events you are organizing or attending
- Promote your seminars and webinars
- Send people to your latest blog post

- Promote others' content, such as blog posts, videos, and podcasts
- Ask a question that could help you solve a problem and engage your network
- Conduct a poll, such as, "How do you like the Google social network?"
- Promote a valued partner by mentioning him and the great products or services he provides (remember that giving first is a key success factor on LinkedIn)
- Tell your network what jobs you have available if you're hiring
- Talk about job fairs you went to if you're job hunting and interviews you had; this will keep your network informed that you are looking for your next big opportunity

What you hope to have happen is that someone will like or comment on your update. This will share the update with that person's network, spreading your message and branding even farther. You can help out the people in your network by liking and commenting on updates you find helpful so the writer gets exposure to your network.

LinkedIn Etiquette Regarding Updates

Here are few pointers to keep in mind to ensure that updates are a valuable part of your LinkedIn activity:

- Limit your updates to a couple a day. This is not Twitter, where multiple posts throughout the day are the norm.
- Restrict your posts to business topics and save personal updates such as where you had lunch and what sitcom you watched for other social networks. Everything you do and say on LinkedIn is branding you. Make sure your status updates reflect the professional brand you want to create.

Clever Ways to Show Up in Network Updates

By updating your status a few times a day, you keep branding yourself. But you don't always have to write a specific status update because you can appear on the home pages of your networks just by being active on LinkedIn as follows:

- Update Your Profile
  Every time you make a change anywhere on your profile, that will show up in your status updates in your first-level connections' pages.
- Make Connections
  Every time you connect with someone, it shows up in the network updates of your connections' home pages. So that's another great reason to build your network.
- Get Active in Groups
  Every time you like or comment on a group post, it shows up in your network's updates.
- Follow Companies
  Go to the top toolbar, click on *Companies* > *Search Companies*, and follow some companies, and it will show up in the updates of your network.

Create a LinkedIn Goal Statement

In addition to the things just mentioned, your daily activities should all serve your purpose for being on LinkedIn. Have you defined what your goals are for being on the site? If not, take some time to write down what you want to achieve in the provided Success Blueprints in Appendix A. Then it will be easy to create activities that naturally support that goal.

For example, here is my LinkedIn goal statement:

I want to be the leading LinkedIn expert, create interest and sales for my social media courses and online trainings, demonstrate my social media expertise, build a worldwide brand, and add value to everyone I meet on LinkedIn.

Create your own goal statement; then get busy doing those things that will help you achieve your outcomes. The next section gives a list of activities you can do every day that will help you.

The big question is, how much time can you devote to LinkedIn? I suggest you put in at least an hour a day if you can. That's the minimum. If you are a commissioned salesperson selling for a company, I would spend four hours each morning networking on LinkedIn and getting to know prospects and then four hours in the afternoon having coffee or phone calls with the people you met. If you are job hunting, I would spend four hours each morning getting to know prospective hiring managers and four hours in the afternoon on calls and informational interviews.

But that's just me, since I love LinkedIn! It's up to you how much time you spend on the site, but remember, the more time you spend, the more results you will get. Again, what you put in you will get out.

Powerful Daily Success Activities

Here are suggestions for activities that will take you to your goals (once they are set):

- Click on the flag icon on the top toolbar to display your notifications. You'll see who has recently connected with you, who's viewed your profile, and so on.
- Reply to all personalized messages in your inbox, and accept all connection requests.
- Answer questions in your field so you become known as the expert.
- Ask a question in the Answers section; this helps establish you as a thought leader. Send thank-yous to people who respond to your question.
- Start discussions in your groups—perhaps a debate on a hot topic that will get lots of input, or a question on something that will help you in your work.
- Respond thoughtfully to group posts with applicable content and not a pitch. The goal is to engage people, not to sell outright.

- Create and distribute content, such as a white paper, a video, or a report to your groups and in your status update. Include a link to your website, if appropriate. Invest a little money (around $100) in a Flip camera, which you can find online on eBay or Amazon.com, to create videos of you and others in your organization to post on YouTube; then attach the URL to that video when you create a post.
- Review the list of groups you belong to, join new groups that will help you achieve your goals, and leave other ones that are not helpful.
- If you have a group, send out invitations every day to your network to get people to join it. Also, send a note to people in your group asking how you can help them.
- Add a new application to your profile that you can use to distribute your content (on the top toolbar, go to *More > Get More Applications*).
- Reach out to people who look interesting and get them to join you on a introductory phone call to find areas where you can help each other.
- Request a recommendation from someone you have worked with.
- Write an unsolicited recommendation for someone who is deserving. There are probably a lot more people in this category than you can recall. Here's a way to jog your memory: go through all your connections in your local area regularly to see whom you have worked with but not yet recommended. The more recommendations you write that are accepted, the more your name and a hyperlink to your profile will appear on other people's profiles.
- Endorse a skill on a first-level connection's profile in his Skills & Expertise section. Your picture with a hyperlink to your profile will now appear on his profile, so that he gets an endorsement of his abilities and you get branding. Write to some trusted friends on LinkedIn and ask for endorsements for some of your skills.
- Check for new potential connections. With more and more people joining every day, it's a good idea to go to *Contacts >*

Add Connections regularly. There you will see whom you know from companies you worked with and fellow alumni whom you can send an invitation to in order to grow your network of first-level connections.

- Search for yourself in the People search in the upper right by typing in the keyword you want to be found for. See where your profile comes up; if you want to be number one, update your profile with keywords and phrases that bring you to number one. This will ensure that opportunities continue to come your way.

- Offer help: when you make a new connection, ask the person, "Is there anything I do to help you?" This might lead to a new opportunity for you.

- Forward introduction requests as soon as you get them, since this is how you would like your requests handled. Also, make unsolicited introductions between connections if you feel they can benefit each other.

- Provide feedback that helps people; it's not necessary to sell anything when you post a comment, since people can always click through to your profile and see what you offer if they have been helped by your comment.

- Thank people who have helped you out with a timely response to your question or your introduction request or who wrote a recommendation for your profile.

- Contact industry leaders and ask if they will be attending an upcoming trade show or conference; if so, see if they have a few minutes to meet with you.

- Invite people that you met at networking events to connect with you. It's a great way to follow up with people and begin a relationship.

- Check your saved searches for companies you are targeting or start a new search. Also check your saved Signal searches for any updates that will present you with opportunities.

- Check out the Advanced People Search to see if there is anyone new matching your target market, and check your saved people searches.

- Check out competitors' personal profiles and company profiles to keep up to date on strategies, products, and services that you may wish to emulate.

Turbocharged LinkedIn Success Activities

As time goes on, your needs with LinkedIn will change. It's a good idea to take a look at all your different options and make sure the site is set up just the way you want it.

- Periodically review the paid accounts and see what they offer. As you get more active with LinkedIn, you may want to get more capabilities in terms of searches and messaging. Go to your name in the upper right, and click on *Settings > Account Type > Compare account types* to see if you are interested in an upgrade. I pay $24.99 a month for the level one premium account, the Business account, and it suits my purposes.
- Check how you are doing in terms of visibility. If you have been optimizing your profile with keywords and engaging lots of people in Groups and Answers, you should be showing up in more and more searches. You can check out how many times you've shown up in searches by clicking on *Home > LinkedIn Home.* Then look on the right-hand side and click on *Who's Viewed Your Profile.* If you are appearing in more and more searches, you're doing good. There really is no number of times you show up in searches that's the best; just make sure your number keeps going up every day.
- Reorder your groups. You want to visit your groups each day and add to the conversations. You may have a set order in which you want to look at them, with groups that have top priority in your daily routine. Since you can join and leave groups at will, your list will eventually not be in the order you want. Go to *Groups > Your Groups* and look for the link that says *Reorder* to the right of *Groups You've Joined.* This will change the order of how they appear when you check on them.

- Check your email settings. You can associate as many emails as you want with your LinkedIn account. This is helpful because some people have had only their work email associated with LinkedIn, and when they lost their job, they found it hard, if not impossible, to get to their LinkedIn account. If you work for someone else, make sure to associate a personal email so you always can get to your account.

Go to your name in the upper right of any screen, click on *Settings*, and then click on *Change* next to where it says Primary Email under your name. That's where you can adjust what emails you have associated with your LinkedIn account and which is the primary one LinkedIn uses to send you information. When you are done, click on *Close*.

That settings box you have opened has a lot of different options. Try clicking around and see how you want to customize your LinkedIn experience now that you have become familiar with the site.

* * *

LinkedIn will reward you with many opportunities and partners from around the world *if* you put in the time. It's such a great resource, I strongly urge you to spend a least an hour a day doing the activities I've outlined and create the success you are seeking. And now—*drum roll!*—I will go to the big finish and pull everything together and inspire you one last time to get active on this amazing site.

Conclusion: Opportunity Is Knocking at Your Door

Your opportunities on LinkedIn are endless. As a professional resource, LinkedIn is growing daily in popularity, which means there are more and more people joining the site who can help you achieve your goals. While it surpasses all other sites in terms of helping you find a job, it's much more than a job search site. LinkedIn is a worldwide database that offers you a wide variety of different opportunities to enhance your business and career depending on your objectives.

To get a read on the diversity of the ways LinkedIn helps people, I took a poll of my network to find out how LinkedIn was assisting them in propelling their businesses and careers. I know you will find the answers inspiring and informative in terms of the diversity of responses:

"A project I was recently on ended earlier than expected and I turned to my network to let them know I was open to consulting opportunities again. I posted a notice that I was available. A few days later a contact from about 15 years ago wrote and said, 'Talk about serendipity! I've been looking to outsource online marketing for my clients.' We are now collaborating on 'white labeling' my services to his clients."

—Maria, Digital Marketing Manager

"I just got off the phone with someone who saw an answer that I posted in the LinkedIn Answer section and decided to call and hire me for a trade show as their booth traffic builder. This has happened many times and would not be possible without social networking."

—Dave, Trade Show Booth Traffic Builder

"I was writing a news release and needed to find a professor at the University of Michigan to get a quote. He was retired and not listed in any directories. By asking for help from members of my U of M Alumni Group I found the connection I needed in just a few hours!"

—Gloria, Media Specialist

"I would say the greatest success would be linking up with the other coauthors of *Improv to Improve Your Business*—a book that was born directly from the LinkedIn Answer section and is now out in the market. I knew none of the other coauthors previously and for me that's where the real magic happens on LinkedIn—the unexpected opportunities that come from broadening your circles."

—Rob, Author

"LinkedIn is an amazing 'poll pool' that features some of the greatest thinkers of our time. I can post a question or poll, and in minutes I can get a feel of what the common and diverse thinking is around the subject matter. It's both exciting and engaging."

—Michael, Leasing Consultant

"I think my biggest success was being able to connect to a key decision maker to discuss a job opportunity via a connection. While I didn't land the opportunity, it did lay the groundwork for establishing a connection that led me to a future opportunity that I landed."

—Sean, Copywriter

"Participation and visibility on LinkedIn has led to qualified leads (10–12 within the past year), many of which I was able to close on the backend. As with many LinkedIn stories, it was not ME going after the leads ... they came to me. At least five were from folks who lurked and watched my activity from a distance. Sometimes our activity on the networks feels like a waste of time. Just remember ... people may still take notice without saying a word! You never know when they'll be ready to make contact!"

—Deana, Content Marketing Innovator

"My biggest success on LinkedIn is probably my starting as a freelance consultant. It was in 2008 and I received a contract on LinkedIn for eight months. I remember at that time that a few of my colleagues met difficult times and were out of work for several months. On my side, I had the contract and so I faced the financial crisis without difficulties. We are still facing difficult and fragile times on the financial and economical level, and LinkedIn remains an essential tool for freelance people like myself."

—Eric, Freelancer

"I joined LinkedIn a very long time ago to find businesses who would want to hire voice talent on my site, Voice123. It took a lot of poking around and talking to related industry folks, but since July 2007 the job-posting average on our site jumped from 700 to 1,500 monthly. The mere growth I found to be an amazing success."

—Steven, Website Manager

Finally, this note from Amnuai in Thailand, who founded Thai Silk Magic and has had success promoting her company:

"As a small handmade Thai silk business located in a remote Thai village with most of us having very limited formal education or opportunities, LinkedIn has been essential to our success.

"By sharing and helping people in various groups and also on Answers, I have had the pleasure to be invited to connect with people who can not only provide me with great advice and support but in quite a few cases they have arranged introductions to leaders in the textiles, fashion, and lifestyle industries.

"This has resulted in some wonderful relationships that have led to five B2B partnerships as well as gaining a wide range of advocates for what we are trying to do for our village. LinkedIn has given me and our Thai village business the opportunity to be able to very successfully compete in a worldwide Thai silk suppliers market that has been dominated by large, well-established, and wealthier competitors.

"People listen and become supporters of our mission of improving lifestyles and education opportunities for the children of our remote Thai village. (We achieve this by sharing all profits.) LinkedIn may well be for business professionals, but success for us is based on the fact that people buy people before anything else."

People Buy People

I could not agree more with Amnuai's assessment. You see, people need to "buy in" to you. Then they will buy from you. If a woman in a small Thai village can use LinkedIn to create success, I believe it has the power to help anyone in the world achieve their goals. It comes down to a magic word: *ask*!

Basically, you need to get active on LinkedIn and ask for what you want, namely:

- Work from a potential client
- An introduction to someone who can assist you
- A job
- Advice
- Attendees for your event
- Publicity coverage
- What else can you come up with? How about a yacht for your next party?

The list is endless and is bounded only by your imagination and desires.

Asking goes hand in hand with another activity on LinkedIn, one that, as you have read, is responsible for many of the opportunities that come your way: give generously to your LinkedIn network! Give by:

- Posting helpful advice and links to great sites in your status updates

- Answering questions
- Joining group discussions with thoughtful replies
- Sending unsolicited recommendations
- Sharing important industry news and updates
- Helping out other users who need advice

So it's a balance. Spend part of your time asking and part of your time giving.

Measure Your Success

After you've taken the time to grow your LinkedIn presence and you are marketing and branding your business and yourself, you should track your progress so you know your efforts are paying off. Since you are investing your time primarily, here are some ways you can tell if your work on LinkedIn is giving you some measure of ROI (return on investment).

How big is your LinkedIn reach?
This is measured by:

- The number of connections you have made
- The number of groups you have joined
- The number of groups you have started
- How many people have joined your groups
- How interactive your groups have become, with people discussing topics and responding on their own

How extensive is your thought leadership?
You can tell by:

- How many questions you have asked
- How many questions you have answered
- How many "best answers" you received
- The number of recommendations you have given
- The number of recommendations you have received

How well have your events and campaigns performed?

If you are posting an event or placing an ad on LinkedIn, take a snapshot of your business before and after so you can measure the effect.

How has your website traffic grown?

Using Google analytics and other measuring services, see how many people are being referred to your site from LinkedIn:

- From your website links in your profile
- From Event postings
- From other places you have put your URL on LinkedIn

Is that traffic growing?

How much new and potential business have you generated?

Track your leads and sales by figuring out:

- How many business leads you have received
- How many phone calls you have generated
- How many face-to-face meetings you have generated
- How many closed deals have resulted

It's Up to You Now

By now you have all you need to begin the process of achieving maximum success on LinkedIn. Remember, what you put into the site you get out of it, so spend time every day getting to know LinkedIn and using it to accomplish whatever it is you want to accomplish. I wish you success in your LinkedIn journey!

Appendix A: LinkedIn
Success Blueprints

If you were going to build your dream house, you wouldn't just hop in your roadster and speed over to Home Depot, buy some random lumber, nails, and fixtures, and rush off to your lot and start banging things together. At least I hope that's not how you would build a house!

No, the first thing you would do is sit down at a drafting table and create a blueprint of the house you want to build. Where do you pour the foundation? Where do the walls go? Where do the kitchen and man cave (if you're a guy) or walk-in closets go? In other words, you create a plan and then execute it. LinkedIn is such an important resource for your success, it pays to do a little up-front planning to ensure that you get the most from this site. The following are 10 Success Blueprints you can use to brainstorm and take notes on what your LinkedIn goals are, what you want your profile to say and how you will make it interactive, whom you want to meet, and what groups you want to join and start.

Take some time and fill in your blueprints. Then use them as notes along your LinkedIn journey.

Success Blueprint #1: Linkedin Goals

What are your goals for being on LinkedIn? Write down as many as you can come up with, such as more customers, referral partners, increased sales, publicity opportunities, freelance work, full-time work, mentors, and investors. Get clear on your goals and that will help you shape your time investment on LinkedIn.

Success Blueprint #2: Branding Yourself

What do you want to be known for? This is essential to figure out so that you can optimize your profile to be found. First, brainstorm on what your brand is: think about what you are good at, what you are known for, and what you like doing.

Success Blueprint #3: Keyword List

You need to use your keywords that describe your brand many times throughout your profile so you are found in LinkedIn searches. As mentioned, this is especially true for your headline, summary, current job, and past jobs. What are your keywords? Brainstorm by answering the following:

What product or service do you sell?

_____

What brand names of products do you sell?

_____

What job responsibilities have you had?

_____

What titles have you had?

_____

What region of the world do you service?

_____

What degrees or certifications do you have?

_____

What software program or other special skills do you have?

_____

_____

_____

_____

Success Blueprint #4: The All-Important Summary

You have 2,000 characters to tell the world about yourself. Write some notes about what you want to say. Who are you? Whom do you help? How do you help people? Why would someone hire you? What's an example of how you were successful? (Do you have an anecdote to tell that you can add to your profile?) What do people like about you?

Who I am:

_____

_____

Whom I help:

_____

_____

How I can help them:

_____

_____

A story or anecdote:

_____

_____

_____

_____

_____

_____

_____

_____

Success Blueprint #5: Specialties— What Sets You Apart

You have 500 characters for specialties. Take some notes on all the things you can do for a client you serve or a company you join. What have you succeeded at in the past? What do people tell you that you're great at? Specialties are usually three to four words. For example, in my field of social media, it could be word-of-mouth marketing or online community management.

Success Blueprint #6: Presentations and Documents

What presentations do you have already on your computer that you can add to your profile using the applications for multimedia? Take an inventory here, then download the free applications by going to *More > Get More Applications*. Read the description of each application, including SlideShare, Portfolio Display, and Box.net, and see which media formats each application supports.

Videos:

_____

_____

PowerPoints:

_____

_____

PDFs:

_____

_____

Presentations:

_____

_____

Artwork:

_____

_____

Multimedia projects:

_____

_____

Success Blueprint #7: Getting and Giving Recommendations

Getting recommendations. Brainstorm about the people you've worked with who you think would give you a recommendation.

I can get recommendations from these people:

_____

_____

_____

_____

_____

_____

Giving recommendations. Often writing an unsolicited recommendation will get you one back. Whom have you worked with that you can recommend? Commit to giving out a few each week.

I can recommend these people:

_____

_____

_____

_____

_____

_____

_____

Success Blueprint #8: Whom Do You Want to Meet?

There are many ways to find people on LinkedIn. The first step is to decide whom you want to meet and think about how that person describes himself or herself. Here is a place to begin to sketch out the profiles of the people you want to meet and how you will find them on LinkedIn.

Target #1

Title: _____

Keywords used to describe himself/herself:

_____

_____

Customer, referral partner, or other:

_____

Industry:

_____

Region:

_____

Types of groups on LinkedIn this person belongs to:

_____

Action steps to meet this person:

_____

_____

_____

_____

_____

(continued)

Target #2

Title: _____

Keywords used to describe himself/herself:

_____

_____

Customer, referral partner, or other:

_____

Industry:

_____

Region:

_____

Types of groups on LinkedIn this person belongs to:

_____

Action steps to meet this person:

_____

_____

_____

_____

_____

_____

_____

_____

Target #3

Title: _____

Keywords used to describe himself/herself:

_____

_____

Customer, referral partner, or other:

_____

Industry:

_____

Region:

_____

Types of groups on LinkedIn this person belongs to:

_____

Action steps to meet this person:

_____

_____

_____

_____

_____

_____

_____

_____

_____

_____

(continued)

Target #4

Title: _____

Keywords used to describe himself/herself:

_____

_____

Customer, referral partner, or other:

_____

Industry:

_____

Region:

_____

Types of groups on LinkedIn this person belongs to:

_____

Action steps to meet this person:

_____

_____

_____

_____

_____

_____

_____

_____

_____

_____

Success Blueprint #9: Joining Groups

You can join up to 50 LinkedIn groups, and I recommend you max out the number. By joining the maximum, you increase your network and the number of people you can reach. You can direct-message anyone in a group where you are a member.

Below you can write down the characteristics of the groups you want to join, then go to *Groups* > *Group Directory* and enter the keywords you've written in different combinations. For example, you can include region and industry, or region and your prospect's job title. Keep experimenting and looking for groups you can join to achieve your goals.

Region I am located in: _____

_____

My professional interest and areas of expertise: _____

_____

_____

Type of products and services I sell: _____

_____

_____

Type of companies I sell to: _____

_____

_____

What companies supply me with: _____

_____

_____

(continued)

Professional titles of my customers:

_____

_____

_____

_____

Professional titles of my vendors:

_____

_____

_____

_____

_____

My hobbies and interests:

_____

_____

_____

_____

_____

Associations I belong to:

_____

_____

_____

_____

_____

Success Blueprint #10: Starting Groups

Write down what kind of groups you may want to start. Use your answers from the last worksheet to create a list of potential groups you can begin by combining keywords from different categories. You can start up to 10 groups and establish yourself as a thought leader while you build a large prospecting database.

My friend runs a company that sells software to corporate sales organizations. His product sends out messages to the company salespeople that reinforce the latest sales training. He manages a group on LinkedIn for Sales and Marketing Vice Presidents that has over 50,000 members; they are precisely his target market, and he's gotten business from the group. What is your target market? And what group will you start for them?

_____

_____

_____

_____

_____

_____

_____

_____

_____

_____

_____

_____

Appendix B: Successful Selling in the Age of Social Media

I enjoy watching the Bloomberg channel on my widescreen TV (when there are no good basketball or football games to watch—one must have priorities), and it's become a habit of mine to tune into the *Bloomberg West* show every night at 6 p.m. to watch an hour of the latest developments in the tech world. Bloomberg gets great guests on the show, from Internet hopefuls to top venture capitalists to Fortune 500 captains of industry, and the one question that they are always asked about the start-up or new website they are discussing is, "Is it a game changer?" In other words, will this new technology change the way we live and work?

I love that term, because it so aptly describes what LinkedIn and all of social media have done in terms of the way we live our lives. Specifically, in terms of the goals of many reading this book, social media has changed the selling game completely. The playing field is now level. No longer do marketers and advertisers stand high up on Mount Olympus shouting down their pitches and laying out their agenda as to what we will buy and how we will buy it. Now buyers are wading chest-deep in and sifting through an avalanche of information in the form of reviews and recommendations from their peers to make their own choices.

The power has swung to the consumer. A survey done in April 2012 by Nielsen, a global provider of consumer research, stated that online consumer reviews are the second most trusted source of

219

information, after word-of-mouth recommendations by friends and family, with a whopping 70 percent of global consumers surveyed saying that they trust this source. In contrast, the survey went on to say that only 47 percent of consumers surveyed trust paid advertising. Said Randall Beard, global head of Advertiser Solutions at Nielsen, "Although television advertising will remain a primary way marketers connect with audiences due to its unmatched reach compared to other media, consumers around the world continue to see recommendations from friends and online consumer opinions as by far the most credible."

The New Five-Step Sales Process

So where does that leave the marketer today? By that I mean, where does it leave *anyone* who attempts to persuade another person to buy something, including entrepreneurs, small business owners, retailers, service providers, and big corporations. You see, everyone is in the same boat: we all have to adopt a new way of selling, and the formula goes like this:

Step 1. Identify your target audience.
Step 2. Identify the needs of your potential clients by learning their hopes, dreams, and fears.
Step 3. Engage with them by listening first and then interacting.
Step 4. Help them with their needs by providing lots of free, valuable resources up front.
Step 5. Offer your product or service once they are in your sphere of influence.

In the new way of marketing, the actual sales offer comes way at the end, after you've created a relationship with the prospect and he or she has come to know, like, and trust you. When you build a relationship first and deliver lots of value in the form of free education or information, the buyer sees you as the preferred provider. Yes, he will still check with his peers for reviews or recommendations, but you're now on his short list or at the top of his list when it comes time to buy. In fact, you may have done such a great job of engagement and building trust that the buyer would not even consider going with anyone else.

I like the way my friend and fellow speaker David T. Fagan describes it when he says we need to completely flip the old model of getting customers first and turning them into fans. In these times we need to make fans first.

"The process of finding new clients and making them raving fans is fading away," Fagan says. "Now we have to make people FANS FIRST and BUYERS SECOND! Crazy I know, but in this new digital age of social media and overall interaction that's exactly what we have to do."

In his very informative book *Likeable Social Media* (McGraw-Hill, 2011), Dave Kerpen agrees with this sentiment:

> By consistently providing great content over time, you won't need to advertise how wonderful you are—your community will already know based on what you've shared. And when they're ready to buy your product or service, they won't need to respond to ads telling them whom to turn to. They won't even need to search Google to find what they're looking for. They'll already feel like they know you—they trust and like you—so they'll turn to you to solve their problem.

Well, how do we make fans first in this new social media–driven model? Basically, by giving to people, adding value to their lives, and serving them, we can then earn the right to interact with them. People prefer to work with givers, not takers.

Put Your Clients' Needs First

When it comes to social media sites like LinkedIn, too many marketers are skipping the first few steps outlined above. They think it's another broadcast medium like radio or TV that just happens to be free. But what you need to do is put yourself in your prospect's shoes. In a general sense, you'd probably agree that people are interested in themselves. There is something they need to achieve—some goal they need to accomplish. What is that goal? What is that need? Focus first on helping them achieve it and you are on solid ground in the new way of selling.

So how do you do that? Well, take an inventory of what you've got that could perhaps fulfill your prospects' needs. What information products have you assembled in the form of ebooks, videos, articles, blogs, interviews, white papers, webinars, and teleseminars? Make sure it's valuable, it speaks to their immediate needs, and it is given to them without expectation of a purchase.

If you help people for free, then how do you eventually sell to them? What you can do is exchange this valuable, problem-solving content in exchange for them opting into your lead capture system. Make use of the various email management programs and set up an opt-in box on your website where prospects exchange their email address for content. Then you can continue to educate, enlighten, and inform them over the weeks and months ahead—building a solid relationship of trust while you add in a soft sell of what you'd like them to purchase.

The Art of Giving

If this sounds like a long, complex process, I'm afraid that you'll just have to get used to it. You can't just barge onto LinkedIn or any other social site and start selling. For example, I have a client who runs a well-known national marketing company. He was unhappy because he was not getting any new clients from his sales efforts on LinkedIn. When I asked what he was doing, he said he was targeting certain types of small business owners—like dentists and chiropractors—and sending them direct unsolicited messages through the LinkedIn system offering his marketing assistance.

That would seem like the logical thing to do, but it does not work. I get four or five direct messages a day on LinkedIn offering some kind of service that are form letters, and I ignore them. You simply can't skip over the engagement process: on LinkedIn you can pull up someone's profile, get to know what she is like, try to ascertain her needs, then offer her some free content rather than just come right out of the gate and try to sell her.

For example, here's how my friend might have handled his messages on LinkedIn for greater results:

> Hi Dr. Smith. I read your profile here on LinkedIn, and I see you have a family dental practice in Smallville. I have helped hundreds of dentists just like you triple their client base in a very short time by leveraging social media. I'd like to send you my free report, "The Top Ten Social Media Strategies for Building Your Dental Practice." There's nothing to buy and no strings attached. So please let me know if I can send it to you. Thanks for your time.

This type of message will get a lot more response. Then my friend could send a report and in the back of the report include a soft sell to the next step in the sales process. He could offer a free, 20-minute phone call to assess where the dentist is in terms of using social media and how social media could be used immediately to help him. If the dentist accepts and engages in the call, now he's pulled into my friend's sphere of influence, and he could potentially be a new client.

Of course, this method is dependent on having a free giveaway. If you don't have any valuable content, either informational or entertainment-oriented, that you can give away, then that's a project for you. Begin to build up valuable resources you can give away for free by listening to the needs of your prospects, then start creating tools and resources to help people achieve their goals. Take advantage of the free polling feature on LinkedIn or use a survey program like SurveyMonkey.com to do your research.

Don't forget the magic word: *repurpose*! You might have created some content already, but it's in another form. You can turn almost anything you've created into free gifts. The speech you gave and recorded can be transcribed and turned into an ebook. You can pull the soundtrack from a video of you and give it away as an MP3 recording. An example of this is when I took many LinkedIn articles I had written over a long span of time and turned them into an instructional ebook that I give away on my site as a free bonus for signing up for my newsletter.

One more thing to consider is that you don't have to build content all by yourself. There are multitudes of professional artists and writers available to help you at affordable rates, and you can find them all on outsourcing sites like Guru.com and Elance.com. I particularly like Elance, and I hire artists from the site all the time to create the professional packaging and polish I need for the online content I create.

Find out what people need and provide it up front for free, and slowly you will create the all-important relationship that affords you trust and credibility and cuts through the noise. By doing that, by being a giver, you will build a following that will become loyal fans and paying clients.

For More Information

Visit www.linkedsuccess.com to:

- Download free resources
- Learn about online LinkedIn training
- Watch video clips
- Subscribe to Dan's newsletter
- Link to other resources from Dan

Connect with Dan at www.linkedin.com/in/linkedinspeaker

Join the conversation by becoming a member of Dan's LinkedIn Group, "Link Success with Dan Sherman"

Contact Dan at dan@linkedsuccess.com to learn more about the services he provides, including:

- Seminars
- Online training
- Corporate training
- Keynotes

Index

A

Accepting Recommendations, 32
Accomplishments for job hunting, 167
Act!, 123
Activities list, daily approach, 191–195
Adding:
    book list apps, 46–47
    connections, 71–72
    Contacts, 67–79
    sections to Profile, 24–27
Advanced keyword optimization strategies, 62–64
Advanced People Search, 82–85
Advanced Profile tips for job hunting, 165–169
Advice from a career coach, 173–176
Alma mater, 8, 54–55, 169
Amazon.com app, 46–47
Android mobile platform, 184–185
Answers, 123–132
    adding Contacts, 75–76
    daily approach, 126
    how to answer questions, 123–126
    job hunting, 157, 171–172
    in Profile, 8

questions:
    asking, 98–99, 126–129
    asking for what you want, 200
    brand yourself with questions, 129–130
    crowdsourcing, 127
    extending, 131
    to find a mentor, 98–99
    how to answer questions, 123–126
    how to ask questions, 127–129
    for mentor recommendations, 97
    sharing, 131–132
    tracking, 130–131
Apple mobile platform, 185
Applications (apps), 42–46, 184–186
Articles, uploading, 45
Asking questions (*see* Answers: questions)
Audio (*see* Multimedia)
Author's contact information, 225–226
Availability for job hunting, 169

B

Beard, Randall, 220
Benefit statement, Profile Information
    box, 11
Birthday, in Personal Information,
    57
Blogs, 11, 42, 74–75
Blueprints (*see* Success blueprints)
Book lists app, 46–47
Box.net, 44–46, 168
Branding:
    Groups, 103–104
    job hunting on LinkedIn, 157
    with questions, 129–130
    success blueprint for, 205
    (*See also* Profile; *specific topics*)
Business cards, public Profile URL
    on, 75

C

Call to action, Profile Summary,
    19–21
Causes I care about, Profile
    Summary, 26
Center of Influence, Contacts, 81
City, Personal Information, 57
Client- and user-focus, 9, 17–18,
    221–222
Closed network, Profile Summary, 19
Colleagues in Experience, adding
    Contacts, 73
College, 8, 54–55, 169
Companies, 139–153
    adding details, 141–144
    contacting, 147–149
    creating an interesting company
        page, 145–146
    creating opportunities with,
        151–152
    daily following, 190
    email communication, 147

    Events, 133–137
    following, 150–151
    introductions, 148–149
    leveraging company information,
        149–150
    listing, 139–141
    Profile elements, 141
    prospecting, 146–147
    recommendations, 143
    Status Updates, 144–145
    (*See also* Job hunting)
Connections:
    Advanced People Search, 83
    Companies, 147–149
    company communication,
        147–149
    daily approach, 190
    Group invitations, 113
    levels overview, 5–6
    other people's connections
        (OPCs), 81–82
    personal, 86–88
    in Profile, 8–9
    reaching first-level, 67–68,
        86–88
    reaching non-first-level, 69,
        88–92
    with strangers, 69
Contacts, adding, 67–79
    500+ as goal, 68–69
    Add Connections, 71–72
    Answer Questions, 75–76
    blogs, 74–75
    Colleagues in Experience, 73
    connecting with strangers, 69
    creative ways, 73–76
    with email, 71–72, 77
    email newsletters, 75
    Groups, 76
    Home: Your LinkedIn Network,
        67–68

how to start inviting contacts, 71–73
invitations, 69–73
Manager's Choice, 76
networking, 74
non-first-level, 73–76
number of first-level, 67–68
open networks, 76–78
People you may know, 72–73
personalized message to request, 74
public Profile URL, 74–75
Report Spam, 70–71
second- and third-level connections, 73–76
sharing, 68–69
TopLinked account, 76–78
websites, 74–75
Contacts:
Advanced People Search, 82–85
Center of Influence, 81
Companies, 147–149
email, 53, 71–72, 77
finding a mentor, 96–102
folks to reach out to, 82
grouping contacts, 94–95
Groups, 104, 109–110
InMail, 88–92, 147–148
introductions, 89–92
making personal connections, 86–88
mass emails as spam, 53
messaging Group members, 109–110
opportunity preference, 55–56
other people's connections (OPCs), 81–82
preferences, 55–56
Profile, 55–57
reaching first-level connections, 15, 34–36, 67–68, 86–88

reaching groups of more than 50 people, 95
reaching groups of people, 92–94
reaching non-first-level connections, 69, 73–76, 88–92
Recommendations, 32, 34–35
Reply Privately, 108
save search, 85–86
settings, 57
Skills endorsements, 52–53
Creating:
Events, 133–135
Groups, 110–112
interesting Company page, 145–146
personalized Recommendation message, 32
Credibility (see Social proof and trust)
Crowdsourcing, 127
Current Experience:
adding Contacts, 73
keyword optimization, 60–61
in Profile, 8
Profile Summary, 21–24
Customizing:
Profile, 15–24
requesting Contact, 74
requesting Recommendation, 32

D

Daily approach, 187–195
Answers, 126
company following, 190
connection making, 190
goal statement, 190–191
Group comments, 190
list of activities, 191–195
Profile updates, 190
Status Updates, 187–190
updating your approach, 194–195

Dancing with Digital Natives (Manafy
    and Gautschi), 158
Demographics of LinkedIn
    members, 4
Details, adding to Companies,
    141–144
Dig Your Well Before You're Thirsty
    (Mackay), 67
Diversifying Groups, 105–107
Documents, success blueprint for, 209

E

E-Bookshelf app, 48
Editing on LinkedIn (*see specific
    topics within major topics, such as*
    Contacts *or* Profile)
Education, 8, 54–55, 169
Elance.com, 224
Email:
    check your settings, 194
    Companies, 147
    Contacts, 53, 71–72, 77
    Group owner, 111
    importing list, to Add Connections,
        71–72
    invite to Connect by individual
        email, 77
    mass emails as spam, 53
    newsletter to add Contacts, 75
    (*See also* Public Profile URL)
Endorsements, Skills & Expertise,
    52–53
Engagement with members, 120,
    220–224
Etiquette:
    Q&A forums, 98–99
    spam, 53, 70–71
    Status Updates, 189
    (*See also* Sharing and giving)
Events, 133–137
    advanced strategies, 136

apps for, 47
    creating, 133–135
    finding a mentor, 99
    measuring success, 201–202
    publicizing, 135–136
Experience:
    adding Contacts, 73
    Colleagues, adding Contacts, 73
    keyword optimization, 60–61
    in Profile, 8
    Profile Summary, 21–24
Export to PDF, Profile, 15
Extending questions, 131

F

Fagan, David T., 221
Fans, growing (*see specific topics*)
Find ability, job hunting, 157
First-level connections:
    number of, 67–68
    reaching, 15, 34–36, 67–68, 86–88
    recommendation requests, 15,
        34–36, 87
Five-step sales process, 220–221
Following Companies, 150–151
Free giveaways, 12–13, 222–224
FTC (Federal Trade Commission), 30

G

Gartner Research, 183
Gautschi, Heidi, 158
Giveaways, 12–13, 222–224
Global reach of LinkedIn, 3–5, 15,
    158
Goals:
    100 percent Profile goal, 7–8
    500+ Contacts, 68–69
    daily approach, 190–191
    goal statement, 190–191
    success blueprint for, 204
    tools for business, 5

Google Alerts, 177
Google professional profiles, 176
Grouping contacts, 94–95
Groups, 103–121
   adding Contacts, 76
   alma mater, 54–55, 169
   announcements, 116
   overview, 103
   brand building with, 103–104
   business building with,
      114–119
   contacts, 104, 109–110
   creating, 105, 110–112, 217
   daily comments, 190
   discussions, 107–108, 120–121
   diversifying, 105–107
   engagement with members,
      120
   finding a mentor, 98
   invitations, 113
   job hunting, 108–109, 157,
      163–164, 170–171
   joining, 104–105, 112,
      215–216
   keyword optimization, 63
   leaving a group, 110
   logo, 111, 119
   Manage, 113–119
   Manager's Choice, 76, 115–116
   member engagement, 120
   members-only, 112
   messaging group members,
      109–110
   name, 111, 119
   navigating, 107–109
   open, 112
   in Profile, 8
   Profile for, 109
   promoting, 108–109, 113–114
   reaching group members,
      109–110
   reaching groups of people, 92–95
   reordering, 194
   searching, 104–106
   settings, 109–110, 115
   starting, 105, 110–112, 217
   statistics, 107
   Subgroups, 114
   success blueprint for joining,
      215–216
   success blueprint for starting,
      217
   templates, 116–119
   types of, 106
   URL for, 113
   Website traffic building,
      120–121
Guru.com, 224

H
Headline:
   for job hunting, 165–166
   keyword optimization, 60
   Profile Information box,
      10–12
Hide Recommendations, 32
Honesty in social media, 2–3

I
Industries, 8, 84
Information box, Profile, 9–15
   benefit statement, 11
   blog, 11
   headlines, 10–12
   language choices, 15
   localized niche, 57
   photograph, 9–15
   public Profile link, 14–15
   Twitter, 13
   website listing, 11–13
Informational interviews, job hunting,
      158

InMail, 88–92, 147–148
Intelligence gathering, Signal,
      180–181
Interests, keyword optimization,
      64
Interview, job hunting, 158, 173
Introductions:
   Companies, 148–149
   Contacts, 89–92
Invitations:
   adding Contacts, 69–73
   email, 53, 71–72, 77
   Groups, 113
   how to start inviting Contacts,
      71–73
   increasing allotment of,
      69–70
   to join LinkedIn, 7
   Profile Summary, 18–20
   Report Spam, 70–71
   View Sent Invitations, 73
   withdraw, 71

J

Job fairs, 170
Job hunting, 155–177
   Answers, 171–172
   Groups, 108–109, 157,
      163–164, 170–171
   Headline, 165–166
   interviews, 158, 173
   vs. job boards, 156–159
   multimedia, 168–169
   premium job listings,
      160–162
   premium services, 172–173
   Profile Summary, 166–167
   recruiter, 155–156
   résumé, 43–44, 168–169
   with Signal, 179–181
   Skills & Expertise, 167

Job Seeker Premium, 172–173
Jobvite, 159
Joining:
   Groups, 104–105, 112,
      215–216
   LinkedIn, 7

K

Kerpen, Dave, 221
Keyword optimization, 59–66
   Advanced People Search,
      82–85
   advanced strategies, 62–64
   Current Experience, 60–61
   Experience, 60–61
   Groups, 63
   Headline, 60
   Interests, 64
   list of, success blueprint for, 206
   moving sections in Profile,
      65–66
   name field Terms and Conditions
      (T&Cs), 64–65
   Past Experience, 61
   Profile, 23–24, 63–64
   public Profile URL, 63
   Recommendations, 63
   research your competition in
      People, 62
   Signal, 179–182
   Skills & Expertise, 64
   Summary, 61
   websites, 63
   when not to optimize, 64–65

L

Languages:
   choices for Profile Information
      box, 15
   spoken by you, in Profile,
      53–54

Lawyer Ratings app, 48
Leaving a group, 110
Legal Updates app, 48
Leveraging company information,
      149–150
Likeable Social Media (Kerpen), 221
LinkedIn:
      Answers, 123–132
      applications (apps), 41–48,
            184–186
      asking questions, 126–130
      benefits of, 4–5
      for business goals, 5
      Company Profile, 139–153
      connection levels, 5–6
      Contacts, 67–79, 81–102
      daily approach to, 187–195
      demographics of members, 4
      Events, 133–137
      give to your network, 200–201
      global reach, 3–5, 15, 158
      Groups, 103–121
      honesty, 2–3
      invitation to join, 7
      job hunting, 155–177
      joining, 7
      keyword optimization, 59–66
      measuring success, 194,
            201–202
      for mobile devices, 183–186
      multimedia applications,
            41–48
      as non-traditional marketing,
            1–6
      opportunity and success with,
            197–202
      paid services (*see* Premium
            account)
      people focus, 2
      Profile (*see* Profile)
      Recommendations, 29–39

      sales with, 219–224
      Signal keywords, 179–182
      success blueprints, 203–217
      testimonials, 197–200
LION, 78
Listing Companies, 139–141
Localized Personal Information,
      57
Logo:
      Company, 141
      Group, 111, 119

M

Mackay, Harvey, 67
Manafy, Michelle, 158
Manager's Choice, 76, 115–116
Managing:
      Groups, 113–119
      Recommendations, 37–38
Marketing, social media as non-
      traditional, 1–6
Mass emails as spam, 53
Maximum Success with LinkedIn
      (Sherman), 46
Measuring success, 194, 201–202
Members of Groups, 109–110,
      112, 120
Mentor, finding a mentor,
      96–102
Miniwebsite (*see* Profile)
Mobile devices, 183–186
      smart phone app, 184
      tablet app, 185–186
      usage statistics, 183
Multimedia:
      apps for, 41–48
      benefits of, 123
      for job hunting, 168–169
Multiple-expertise promotion, Profile
      Summary, 19–21
My Travel By TripIt app, 48

N

Name:
    Group creation, 111, 119
    Groups, 111, 119
    keyword optimization, 64–65
    Terms and Conditions (T&Cs),
        64–65
Navigating Groups, 107–109
Needs:
    of client focus, 9, 17–18, 221–222
    identify, for mentor, 97
Networks:
    adding Contacts, 74
    closed, 19
    mentors, 97–98
    open, 12, 19, 37, 76–78
New Yorker, 29
News, Signal, 179–182
Newsletter to add Contacts, 75
Nielson, 219–220
Non-first-level connections, reaching,
    69, 73–76, 88–92
    (*See also* Second- and third-level
        connections)
Notifications, Recommendations,
    32–34

O

Open networks:
    adding Contacts, 76–78
    Groups, 112
    Profile Summary, 18–20
    Recommendations, 37
Opportunities:
    with Companies, 151–152
    Contacts preference, 55–56
    with LinkedIn, 197–202
Order of jobs, Profile Summary,
    23–26
Organizations I support, Profile
    Summary, 26

Other people's connections (OPCs),
    81–82

P

Paid services (*see* Premium account)
Parinello, Anthony, 174–175
Past Experience keyword
    optimization, 61
PayPal, for recurring LinkedIn
    expenses, 78
PDFs, uploading, 15, 44–45
People:
    Advanced People Search,
        82–85, 97
    keywords, research your
        competition, 62
    recommending people you know,
        36–37
    success blueprint for targeting,
        211–214
    you may know, adding Contacts,
        72–73
Personal Information, Profile, 57
Phone number, Personal
    Information, 57
Photos:
    Profile Information box, 8–15
    Skills endorsements, 52–53
Poll app, 42, 47–48
Portfolio Display app, 48
PowerPoint slides, uploading, 44
Preferences, Contacts, 55–56
Premium account:
    Advanced People Search, 83
    InMail, 88–92, 147–148
    job listings, 160–162
    Job Seeker Premium, 172–173
    saving contact searches, 85
    Toplinked account, 77–78
Presentations, success blueprint for,
    209

Product promotion, 45, 146
Profile, 7–27
  100 percent Profile goal, 7–8
  book lists, 46–47
  client-and user-focus of, 9,
    17–18
  Company, 139–153
  completing, 7–8
  Contacts, 55–57
  customizing, 15–24
  daily updates, 190
  Education, 8, 54–55, 169
  export to PDF, 15
  finding a mentor, 100
  Group Profile, 109
  Information box, 9–15
  keeping current, 100–101
  as key to networking, 8–9
  keyword optimization, 23,
    59–66
  languages spoken by you,
    53–54
  measuring success, 194
  moving sections in Profile,
    65–66
  multimedia, 41–48
  Personal Information, 57
  polishing, 51–58
  recommendation requests, 15
  scannable, 9, 17–18
  sections added to, 24–27
  Skills & Expertise, 51–53
  social proof, 52
  Summary, 16–28
  using first person, and humanizing,
    174
  View Profile, 15, 53
Promoting your Group, 113–114
Prospecting Companies, 146–147
Public Profile URL, 14–15, 63,
    74–75

Publications, Profile Summary,
    26–27
Publicizing Events, 135–136
Pull medium, social media as, 3

Q
Questions (see Answers: questions)

R
Reach:
  global reach of LinkedIn,
    3–5, 15
  measuring success, 194, 201
Reaching people (see Contacts)
Reading list app, 46–47
Real Estate Pro app, 48
Recommendations, 29–39
  accepting, 32
  Advanced People Search, 83
  chose position for
    recommendation, 31–32
  Companies, 143, 146
  deciding who to ask, 32
  from Education, 54
  hiding, 32
  keyword optimization, 63
  know who you are recommending,
    36–37
  managing, 37–38
  notification in Inbox, 32–34
  opening, 37
  personalized message to request,
    32
  preparing to get, 31–32
  request a new recommendation,
    15, 31–37, 87
  request a revised recommendation,
    32–33, 37
  sending draft recommendation,
    33–34
  sharing and giving, 34–35, 38

Recommendations (*Cont.*):
  Skills endorsements, 52–53
  as social proof, 29–31, 38–39,
    220
  success blueprint for, 210
  unsolicited, for others, 36
  writing for others, 34–35, 38
Recruiters, job hunting, 155–156,
  164–165
Referrals, job hunting, 158
Relationship building (*see* Contacts;
  specific topics)
Relevance, Advanced People Search,
  83
Report Spam, 70–71
Repurposed content as giveaway,
  223–224
Research:
  competition in People, 62
  for job interview, 173
Résumé, 43–44, 168–169

S

Sales and selling, 181, 219–224
Scannable Profile, 9, 17–18
Schawbel, Dan, 158–159
School, 8, 54–55, 169
Search:
  Contacts, 82–86
  Groups, 104–106
  for a skill, 52
Second- and third-level connections:
  adding Contacts, 73–76
  personalized message to request,
    74
  reaching, 69, 88–92
Selling to VITO (Parinello), 174–175
Settings:
  Contacts, 57
  email, 194
  Groups, 109–110, 115

Sharing and giving:
  adding Contacts, 68–69
  endorsements, Skills & Expertise,
    52–53
  free giveaways, 12–13, 222–224
  questions, 131–132
  Recommendations, 34–35, 38
  with your network, 200–201
Signal, 179–182
  intelligence gathering,
    180–181
  for job hunting, 179–181
  for marketing, 181
  for sales, 181
Silverstein, Lee, 173–176
Sitewire, 183
Skills & Expertise:
  adding a skill, 51–52, 55
  endorsements, 52–53
  for job hunting, 167, 175
  keyword optimization, 64
  Profile, 51–53
  search for a skill, 52
SlideShare app, 43
Smart phones, LinkedIn mobile app
  on, 184
Social influence circle (*see* Contacts)
Social media:
  as marketing revolution, 1–2
  as non-traditional marketing,
    1–6
  Profile Information box, 13
  as pull medium, 3
  (*See also* LinkedIn; *specific topics*)
Social proof and trust:
  job hunting on LinkedIn, 157
  Profile, 52
  Recommendations, 29–31, 38–39,
    220
  word-of-mouth recommendations,
    220

Spam, 53, 70–71
Specialties:
   job search, 172
   Profile Summary, 19–21
   success blueprint for, 208
   (*See also* Skills & Expertise)
Spell-check of Profile Summary, 21
Status Update:
   Companies, 144–145
   daily approach, 187–190
   etiquette, 189
   job hunting on LinkedIn, 157
   in Profile, 8
   sharing, 187–188
Subgroups, 114
Success blueprints, 203–217
   branding yourself, 205
   goals, 204
   for joining Groups, 215–216
   keyword list, 206
   presentations and documents, 209
   recommendations, 210
   specialties, 208
   for starting Groups, 217
   summary, 207
   targeted people, 211–214
Success with LinkedIn, 197–202
Summary, Profile, 16–28
   overview, 16–18
   call to action inclusion, 19–21
   causes I care about, 26
   client- and user-focus, 17–18
   invitations, 18–20
   job hunting, 166–167
   keyword optimization, 61
   multiple-expertise promotion, 19–21
   open *vs.* closed networks, 19
   order of jobs, 23–24
   organizations I support, 26
   publications, 26–27

specialties, 20–21
success blueprint for, 207
volunteer positions, 22–23, 25
writing and spell-check, 21

T
Tablets, LinkedIn mobile app on, 185–186
Targeted people, success blueprint for, 211–214
Testimonials on Company page, 146
Third-level connections (*see* Second- and third-level connections)
Thought leadership, measuring success, 194, 201
TopLinked account, 76–78
Tracking questions, 130–131
TripIt app, 48
Trust (*see* Social proof and trust)
Twitter, 13

U
University, 8, 54–55, 169
Updates (*see* Status Update)
Upgraded services (*see* Premium account)
Uploading:
   articles, 45
   email lists, 71–72
   PDFs, 15, 44–45
   PowerPoint, 44
   video, 43–44
URL for Group, 113
URL for public Profile, 14–15, 63, 74–75

V
Video, uploading, 43–44
View Profile, 15
View Sent Invitations, 73
Volunteer positions, Profile Summary, 22–23, 25

W

Websites:
  adding Contacts, 74–75
  Groups, 120–121
  keyword optimization, 63
  LinkedIn as mini, 7–27
  measuring success, 202
  Profile Information box, 11–13
  traffic building, 120–121, 202
Word-of-mouth recommendations,
  220
WordPress, 42

Work experience (*see* Experience)
Writing:
  to first-level connection, 87
  Profile Summary, 20–21
  Recommendations, 34–35, 38
  (*See also specific topics*)

Y

You Can Be a Peak Performer!
  (Sherman), 46

Z

Ziglar, Zig, 3

About the Author

Dan Sherman is a LinkedIn expert, social media marketing coach, author, and speaker whose focus is teaching business professionals how to leverage the incredible power of LinkedIn. Through his company Linked Success, Dan shows entrepreneurs, business owners, and professionals how to get more customers, sell more products, build a powerful brand, and establish themselves as thought leaders by using LinkedIn every day.

Dan has more than 20 years of marketing management experience. He served as director of marketing for two Silicon Valley Internet companies, where he led marketing teams and developed innovative sales-generating programs. Dan was also a manager at Charles Schwab for eight years, where he created the marketing programs for the fastest-growing department in Schwab's history, which brought in $50 billion in assets. He is an avid entrepreneur, and after leaving the corporate world, he built several successful Internet businesses.

Dan is a highly rated speaker, and his social media and Internet marketing seminars receive top accolades from both new and veteran online marketers. He is a LinkedIn blogger for an internationally known marketing site, and he has contributed articles on sales to *Entrepreneur* and *Selling Power* magazines. He graduated from Tufts University in Medford, MA, with a BA in English with honors. Dan is the author of *You Can Be a Peak Performer!* and creator of the online training courses *Linked Into Action* and *Affiliate Wealth Today.*

Dan's LinkedIn resource site can be found at www.LinkedSuccess .com. His LinkedIn profile is at www.linkedin.com/in/linkedinspeaker. Dan's Twitter name is @DanLinkedInMan. Dan's two LinkedIn groups are "Tampa Bay Marketing Professionals," with over 3,700 members, and "Link Success with Dan Sherman."

YOU CAN BE A PEAK PERFORMER!
10 STEPS TO UNLIMITED SUCCESS WHICH ANYONE CAN TAKE

"I think your ideas are wonderful and I am sure your book will continue to prove very helpful to many people."—Anthony Robbins, author, *Awaken the Giant Within*

"This remarkable book is a real springboard to greater success and achievement. It will change the way you think and everything you do. It's great."—Brian Tracy, author, *Goals! How to Get Everything You Want—Faster Than You Ever Thought Possible*

This book will show you how to apply the strategies of today's peak performers directly to your quest for success. From Bill Gates to Oprah Winfrey, from Charles Schwab to Debbie Fields, the secrets of over 80 peak performers—all millionaires and billionaires—are revealed. You'll learn how to:

- Think and act like a peak performer
- Push through any fears blocking your unlimited success
- Transform limiting beliefs into unstoppable self-confidence
- Turn obstacles into business opportunities
- Create million-dollar business ideas
- Live your dreams

If you have always wanted to be rich, you'll want to study the stories in this book about mega-wealthy individuals who started with nothing and became superstars. You'll learn that you can have that kind of success too. All you need to do is model the strategies of the world's most successful people described in this book, and with perseverance you too can create any kind of life you want.

Available from www.Amazon.com
Paperback, 216 pages: $14.95
Kindle version: $9.00
  ISBN-10: 1452879443
  ISBN-13: 978-1452879444

LINKED INTO ACTION

LinkedIn is the world's largest professional networking site online, with over 175 million professionals and growing fast. Now is the time for you to join LinkedIn, tell the world about your business, and set yourself apart from your competition. And with LinkedIn, for the first time in history, you can bypass all gatekeepers and get right to the decision maker who is in a position to buy from you or hire you.

With over six hours of easy-to-follow video instruction, Linked In to Action is the number one tool for learning how to master Linked-In to achieve all your business and professional goals. This online video course is carefully constructed to take you step-by-step through the process of branding yourself and connecting with the professionals who will be your next customers and partners.

Specifically, you will discover how to get more leads, more sales, and more traffic to your website. You will learn how to create a powerful brand that will pull opportunities to you. You'll discover how to network with partners, investors, advisors, and other professionals who can take your career to the next level. And if you are job hunting, you'll learn how to directly contact hiring managers and recruiters who are in a position to offer you work immediately.

Take control of your future, and master LinkedIn with the #1 road map to success: Linked Into Action! Visit:

www.LinktoAction.com

Also by Dan Sherman

AFFILIATE WEALTH TODAY

Every day people look at the tremendous growth of the Internet and wonder how they can get involved and make money. With over 2 billion people worldwide now online, Internet marketing is only getting bigger and bigger. If you want to learn how to generate income online with no product, no experience, and no investment, you need to consider affiliate marketing.

Affiliate marketing is *not* Multi Level Marketing (MLM) or network marketing. In affiliate marketing, you are an independent contractor marketing other people's products online. You work for yourself, and you don't recruit people or build an organization. You work in conjunction with leading companies whose products you market online. Affiliate marketing allows you to get into business for yourself with no start-up costs, work with well-known companies and brand names, choose your products, and build an additional stream of income or full-time work.

Dan Sherman is an affiliate marketing expert, and he offers a home study course especially created for those new to affiliate and Internet marketing. It consists of over 20 videos and numerous ebooks that are instantly available to you once you purchase the course. Learn at your own pace in the comfort of your home exactly how to start your own successful online business. Visit:

www.AffiliateWealthToday.com

THIS IS MY BILLBOARD

HEADLINE [the GDI

CONTACT → PORTFOLIO URL (BEHANCE) ✓

SUMMARY - WHAT I DO AND THE SERVICE I PROVIDE.   KEYWORDS ✓

RECOMMENDATIONS - ASK   - WRITE. - KEN EULIE
                                         - ANNE

DESIGN SPEAL -
        "WHAT BUSINESS AM I IN" - 2 SENTENCES OR LESS.
SEND OUT A NOTICE. TO CONNECTIONS.
        DESCRIPTION:

PORTFOLIO HOME ICON
    - [get]   - AM I USING BEHANCE ✓
                    PROPERLY.

PAGE BANNER
    - BEST REPRESENTATION OF WHAT I DO.
        - LOGO PATTERN
        - JAPANESE PRODUCT LIST / IMAGE | PATTERN

WHAT GROUPS WOULD I WANT TO BE A PART OF.
        ✓ RED DOT
        - DESIGN MINDS
✓ KEYWORDS : VISUAL DESIGNER, GRAPHIC ARTIST, BRAND DESIGNER
            CREATIVE! ART DIRECTION.

4 KEY PLACES
FOR KEYWORDS
────────────
    PG. 60

JOB SEEKING GROUPS